Life with GBM Brain Cancer
Blessing in Disguise
My Store of survival of over six years!

A subsequent edition of Life with GBM Brain Cancer (My Story and other Essays) published on Amazon in May 2018.

Table of Contents

Dedicated to

All the Cancer patients of the world and their carers!

With Special Thanks to:

To my courageous wife Anu Singh,
Who always stood with me in thick and thin.
And my angelic children Zoravar Singh and Nimrat Singh,
Who kept me in high spirits with their adorable acts and talks.

The woods are lovely, dark and deep,
But I have promises to keep,
And miles to go before I sleep,
And miles to go before I sleep.

- *Robert Frost (1874 – 1963)*

Dream is not the thing you see in sleep,
but is that thing that doesn't let you sleep.

- A.P.J. Abdul Kalam (1931- 2015)

Prologue

All the art of living lies in fine mingling of
letting go and holding on
- Havelock Ellis

.

We say that life is always full of ups and downs. We also say that for some people, these 'ups' and 'downs' could be relatively trivial but for some, these can turn out to be significant events that can severely batter them and change their lives dramatically. Whether life changes for good or for worse, depends upon many factors and one of the key elements is the attitude towards life that the person holds or acquires during this period of radical transition.

This book is an 'excerpt' from the story of my life, an excerpt of almost six years. Six years of a journey of ups and downs – of holding on to things that mattered to me and letting go off things that I had no control over.

We all go through the rough patches in our lives and if you

13

look around and without venturing too far, you will find plenty of such examples. Maybe it was you who has suffered some pain in your life, or it might have been your loved one who could be suffering or had endured pain in the past.

Whoever undergoes some sort of suffering or pain (be it physical or mental), it is normal to experience extremely conflicting thoughts and experiences. The pain could be due to 'physio-psychic' setbacks such as critical illnesses, wars, terror attack, huge financial loss, major accident or other unfortunate events.

Also, the suffering could also be caused by big 'emotional hurts' as well, such a betrayal in love and relationship, betrayal by business partner after establishing a successful venture, not being able to fulfill the desires that the person always aspired for or not been able to achieve aims/goals that the person truly wanted to achieve etc. All these sufferings are not only potentially heart breaking and morale crushing events, but sometimes, they could prove to be fatal as well.

Of course, there are times when a person does not get any chance to "experience" these ups and downs at all, and unfortunately, the person is decimated without any forewarning such as tragic deaths in war, in terrorism act, fatal accident, strokes, heart attacks etc. These are situations where a person does not even get any chance to take another breath, leave alone a chance to re-direct the future or learn from the past. Clearly nothing can be done in these most unfortunate conditions, which are the truly the scariest tragedies of humanity since time immemorial.

Yet, we cannot deny that often we do come across situations, where life does provide a second chance to us. Sometimes life can hammer us and crush us but still spare us. The suffering or the pain that one had endured in the past had been clearly out of person's control but the person's attitude, and willingness to strengthen it further during the 'current suffering' determines the future of the person and how the person faces the challenge that life has thrown at her/him. I am sure you too must have seen or read about such examples and often wondered what superhuman effort might have inspired such individuals.

Stating again, my understanding is that one of the prime determining factors in facing adversity is the person's attitude towards life, and the desire to live, which is inherent and quite opposite to intentionally or unintentionally conditioned thinking of inviting suffering or at an extreme, to be suicidal. Often these difficult situations can trigger either the self-harm tendencies in a person or on the other extreme may fill the person with a new impulse to live, survive and thrive. When the person aims to re-live the life with full zest, I call it re-birth within one 'biological' span of life.

In my case, it was an upheaval that shocked me in middle of 2015, and yet within two years I got fully exhausted and was pushed to despair completely. I was diagnosed and operated upon for the Brain Cancer, which later turned out to be the deadliest cancer known to humankind- GBM (Glioblastoma Multiform). For weeks after my initial diagnosis, I was extremely scared because death seemed imminent to me. Then, I had no option but to lift myself up and turn my thinking upside down. The internal struggle to believe in living instead of dying before living my life was immense, a belief that soon became my desire and then an obsession.

My fear dissolved when it was established to me that I am going to survive, at least for now and it became my priority to find reasons to live life in my situation.

During the first three years since the diagnosis of my illness, I lived many lives in parallel. These years had rendered me disabled; I had lost my job and stopped earning for my family. Even worse, I lived a life of extreme morbidity and real prospects of mortality.

Yet, since no official prognosis was made in my case by my doctors, I also lived a life hoping for survival, gaining strength and organizing thoughts of love, forgiveness and general positivity amidst all the melancholy.

Life Prepares You

History and even the present world are full of examples where on the face of adversity ordinary people have bounced back to emerge stronger and victorious; or in contrary some have drowned away completely never to emerge back to see the light of life ever again. None of these people would have pre-experienced what they were about to go through. Instead, during their crisis, they could only draw from whatever 'reservoir of spirit' they had filled during their pre-crisis life span. It all depends how the sufferer had lived her/his pre-crisis life, whether s(he) filled the reservoir, with positive strengthening thoughts or negative weakening thoughts. It is this spirit that determines the future approach and hence set the people apart. If you happen to be fortunate enough not to have been surprised by life yet, then my recommendation is not to wait for that to happen and start filling the reservoir of your spirit with positive strengthening thoughts and stop entertaining or establishing a pattern of negative weakening thoughts. Let me be brutally honest here– life spares no one and it tests all of us sooner or later. So just be prepared! If you stay prepared for worse, you will enjoy your life fully and without fear. The aim is not to drag too much into doom and gloom of negative speculations. We approach the day hoping for the best and work for the best and yet stay prepared for the worst. When a person is thus ready to face any situation of life, bright or grim, with grace, it determines their approach. I call it 'courage'.

In pre-crisis life, if on day-to-day basis, one can manage not to get indulged into unfavorable 'negative' thoughts then there are always positive strengthening experiences or actions, albeit at smaller levels. This self-training in dealing with trivial issues of life prepares a person capable of handling bigger issues that the person may encounter. It is very much like training a little bit regularly, to eventually build physical strength over the long run. During a normal living, it is also a matter on focusing and appreciating what a person does have, rather than constantly complaining about the have nots.

During the downward slope of these events, one world is destroyed and if the person keeps courage and had kept the reservoir of thoughts filled with positive strengthening thoughts, this downward slope doesn't last long and soon starts to take an upward turn, but the key words are 'positive attitude' and 'courage' here. But if the on the other hand, a person had filled the reservoir of spirit with negative weakening thoughts throughout their life, then the person often sinks at the most challenging events of life, and the downward trend continues resulting in the defeat of the person's spirit first and followed by death often much before his/her destined time.

These different understandings set the people apart. One set gathers all essential strength to overcome the challenges that the life has always thrown and yet another set falls deep into the dark chasm where there is nothing, but dark thoughts driven by fears and insecurities.

However, I must clarify that thinking of the past moments that gave us strength, happiness and serenity are good and they are important for the development of self as well and contribute towards our love for living life. Not to mention these good memories bring clarity to rest of the life that lies ahead of us. If we opt to realize the positivity in these past challenging moments, they often help us develop our capacity in enduring pain and suffering. Once that clarity is formed, then the person does not regret how short or long the rest of the life turn out to be. The person just becomes bold enough to face the reality.

- - - - --

During suffering, we walk a path that has often been walked by others. We can educate ourselves by learning from their struggles, suffering and pain and explore their memoirs and stories to walk on the same path, correct our attitude if needed, and explore the meaning of our own existence and dig deeper within ourselves to explore in our own spirit for the answers to the questions like – "What should be, or should have been the purpose of my living?" or "What are my deepest and most paramount desires that can tempt me to keep living on?" and "Who do I owe my life to and why must I keep living on for that person(s)?". By doing this we fill our own reservoir of spirit with strengthening positive attitudes.

Then this reservoir full of positive attitudes becomes the essence of our individual being. Finally, this makes us join the path that other have travelled before us.

Life can surprise you

When I was diagnosed with the Brain Cancer, I was halfway on my learning process. I was half strong and half weak. I had to some extent been filling the reservoir of my spirit with positive strengthening thoughts, but it was by no means completely filled yet. Hence on my diagnosis, when I speculated that my remaining lifespan could be as short as few months, I suffered from one big fear and two terrible regrets.

The Fear: The fear was obvious. It was a fear of imminent death and especially after having read the statistics published on the Internet such as this one from by the American Brain Tumor Association or ABTA[1] :

As of early 2018:

"For adults with more aggressive glioblastoma, treated with concurrent Temozolomide and radiation therapy, median survival is about 14.6 months and two-year survival is 30%. However, a 2009 study reported that almost 10% of patients with glioblastoma may live five years or longer."

And, as of mid 2019

"For patients with IDH (Isocitrate dehydrogenase) mutant glioblastoma, the prognosis is significantly better (median survival of

---

[1]http://www.abta.org/brain-tumor-information/types-of-tumors/glioblastoma.html

*27 – 31 months) compared to IDH wildtype (the one I had)
glioblastoma (median survival 11-13 months) after diagnosis.".
"IDH wildtype glioblastoma occurs in about 90% of GBM brain
tumours and usually indicates that the tumour formed as glioblastoma
since the very beginning (primary GBM) and carries a worse
prognosis than those classified as being IDH mutant".[2]*

Clearly, the information was genuine, and it started to
cause extreme distress to me, my wife Anu and our
families back in India. Even if I was to be extremely lucky
and to be in the luckiest 10% of the patients, practically I
had abysmally low chances of surviving beyond five years.

Regret 1: I had a young family and I had always loved
everyone immensely – my wife Anu, my seven-year-old
son Zoravar and three-year-old little daughter Nimrat at
the time of my diagnosis. My regret was leaving them all
alone in the big wild world and not been able to fully
secure them before I depart.

---

[2] https://www.braintumourresearch.org/info-support/types-of-brain-tumour/glioblastoma-multiforme

Regret 2: The second regret on the face of death was that I could not do anything significant with my life, when I had so many dreams and desires. I had taken life for granted as if it was a never-ending adventure. I somehow had this in my mind somewhere that I am going to live for 100 years. I would always think and if I keep myself physically fit and mentally alert, then during that span, I should be able to do something worthwhile. I had effectively wasted the most precious years of my life in those illusions and in 'drifting'.

And now, the deadly trident with one prong of fear and two prongs of regrets, and of imminent death hanged over me. It was killing me before time. It scared me and made me afraid all the time. I knew even if don't die of my illness in next few weeks, I would die of the distress.

The Sudden Awakening

Though I had never experienced it, but it is my personal belief again that in Near-death Experience (NDE), just when the person is about to die, s(he) is pulled back to life by some force and I think that pull is inside the person itself and not anywhere outside. That force has to be from the reservoir of the spirit, filled with positive strengthening thoughts.

In such extreme situations, sometimes strange kind of awakening happens to us and all of a sudden, we are forced to change the direction of our thinking. I am not going to speculate too much as to what causes this, but my understanding is that even when a person is close to death, at least some good thoughts and wishes must stay with that person, and at times pulls him(her) back from the jaws of death.

Not NDE, but I too had a very strange kind of awakening and a 'pull back'.

A day later, when I was discharged from the hospital after the brain surgery in Fortis, Chandigarh, I was finding very difficult to go to sleep. When in middle of the night, I was half awake and half drugged, a hallucination (Delirium) originated from my unconscious mind and suggested to me that I must utilize my remaining time as effectively as I could, because remainder of my life could last just few weeks. That was a small but the first spark of 'positive' thinking that originated in my 'unconscious' and 'ill' mind. But I utterly lacked any will to lift myself up and kept lying in my bed thinking consciously – "what's the point? I am not going to survive anyway beyond a few weeks. Let me just prepare myself to embrace a peaceful death, because it could knock my door anytime". I embraced that thought and drifted myself to a somber mood – but there was no sign of sleep.

My fears were clearly bringing me much closer to my end, yet something in my mind that kept nudging me. On the same occasion, my delirium continued: "OK. If you are really departing then before dying, at least do something for your wife and for your children". That thought proceeded with a vivid scene that I am in front of my lawyer in London and writing my will. The second scene was: I was telling my children, about toughest reality ever of their lives that "you must not expect that you father is going to survive for too long" and I apologized to them for not been able to do much for them while I lived.

The unconscious positive thinking originated because I have been filling the reservoir of my spirit with positive strengthening thoughts and on the other hand my conscious negative thinking was there because the reservoir of my spirit was not completely full yet, it contained negative weakening thoughts and emotions.

I couldn't sleep that night till the early hours of the morning when the birds began their chirping, which finally gave me some calm.

When eventually I managed to get some sleep, may be for a couple of hours, I woke up with shock of what I had been hallucinating about during the night. That sudden realization made me even more sad and made me cry. I must have wept for over an hour, quietly, under my blanket. I did not want to die and wanted those deliriums to go away forever.

Later in the morning, mother asked me how my sleep has been. I just told her that I could not sleep well and have been getting some negative thoughts. She looked concerned and told me she will speak to my doctors so that I sleep well. By night, my parents were around me, ready with sleeping pills. I felt I had no options and started to take the pills every night and would drift off to sleep, effectively without indulging into any negative thoughts.

The deliriums stopped and since I was getting good sleep the insane thoughts were finally over as well. During the day, I began to feel positive energy again. I stopped being a sorry person and 'consciously' vowed to stay brave till the last moment I am alive.

During the day, I began to take some more rest and found that in the daytime, my thoughts were more objective and generally positive, because I was conscious enough and awake to reason and direct my thinking towards positivity. During the daytime, by conscious thinking I made a plan to go back to London and with my lawyer write my will and secure the future of my children. I discussed this with Anu, and she agreed with me completely. Even though, it wasn't strictly a legal necessity because by default my house would have gone to Anu anyway, but I still wanted to do it for my own peace of mind. Since Anu was also bearing mental and physical torture with me, she too wanted to make her own will.

With that resolution, I had strengthened my spirit and had 'consciously' prepared myself to face whatever verdict destiny was to bestow upon me. If I had continued with my pessimist thinking of the reservoir that was filled with the negative weakening thoughts, I could have easily drifted towards death.

When did my fears shed and when did the faith took over my spirit, I do not remember. But what I do know that it has been the positive strengthening attitude that I had always preferred and had always been on alert not to let in any negative weakening attitude in my mind.

Conclusion

Whatever happened to me during the period of my illness and whatever path I had travelled during that phase of my life, I have tried to capture in this book. These excerpts, I hope, will provide some insight as how I managed to achieve such a state of mind amidst all uncertainties of life that stayed with me to scare me every night, for almost six now as of the summer of 2021.

The book is divided into two parts:

Part 1 narrates my journey through the deadliest Brain Cancer, GBM (Glioblastoma Multiform) and how I have managed to survive so far. Clearly, this part is very specific to me and is essentially a timeline of the events of my illness, treatment and resulting scans so far. It elaborates on the symptoms that I had ignored early on, my diagnosis, treatment so far, my suffering during the treatment and finally how I gathered my strength and desire to live with the support of my family and for my family – my wife Anu, my son Zoravar and my daughter Nimrat.

Part 2 of the book comprise of essays that I had complied during my illness, as I was researching to find cure, if any, for my disease. I was doubtful whether any cure was available for this disease, because of very low survival rate of the patients, who suffer from it. I tried to keep this part generic but couldn't help myself giving a GBM specific skew to it.

Even though the Brain Cancer patients and their carers are

likely to get more benefit by reading this part, but I hope it should be able to give some essential tips to the patients suffering from other neurological conditions as well such as Alzheimer, Epilepsy, Multiple sclerosis, Parkinson's, Migraines etc. Moreover, this part, hopefully, should also benefit the patients and caretakers of other types of cancers as well.

With Best Wishes

Satinder Singh
31/08/2021
London

Part 1 My Story

Event Timeline

In Part 1 of this book, I would like to tell my story how I lived my life while suffering from the deadliest Brain Cancer called Glioblastoma Multiform or simply GBM. Also, I would like to share some glimpse from my personal and family life of the turns and twists and where I got immense support and encouragement from my family.

Background

.

By middle of the year 1999, I had acquired decent set of skills to make a good 'material' success in the world. I was equipped with an Engineering degree in 'Electronics', and an MBA in 'International Business'. Along with them I had some key certifications in software - at my own effort. I was confident about my capabilities to build a decent future for myself; in fact, I was so sure that when I mastered the new programming language Java, I just wanted to satiate the burning desire of using all my qualifications in synergy. I did not even bother to join the commodity trading job; I had secured during my campus placement of MBA. Instead, I wanted to go the e-commerce way, that was promising a new world and endless possibilities of creativity in the future ranging from online shopping malls (such as Amazon) to Artificial Intelligence or just AI. I recall, once my father complemented that "with qualifications like Java certification with Masters in International Business, you can write your own destiny".

My 'hunger' was to take risk by trying out software and build some kind of magical systems with big software houses of the world such as Sun Microsystems or Oracle, the leading global corporations at that time.

In the mid of year 2000, I arrived in London and started to work on the Information Technology (IT) projects that IBM offered to me, and these projects were in financial markets sector, my field of studies during the MBA. That was a perfect start to my career and exactly what I wanted.

I was engaged to my fiancée Anu and was immensely in love with her. In London, I started to work very hard on the demanding projects and Anu would call me and wake me up every morning to give a fresh start to my day. It was a great time of my life – a great job with promising career and my love across half of the world waiting for me; and I was restless all the time to bring her over to London with me. Finally, the wait ended in November 2000 when we got married and Anu joined me in London just couple of weeks before the Christmas.

But the hectic lifestyle of London and hours of traveling in the underground trains was no charm. Few weeks later in January 2001, through IBM only, I relocated myself to Norwich in East Anglia and both of us worked in the head office of AVIVA, one of the leading global insurers. While I was working in the software development of the company through IBM, Anu got a job directly with them in customer services area. We stayed in Norwich till middle of year 2005, where we bought our first house and car, and after finishing our extended honeymoon of around 5 years, we decided to come back to London. I joined RBC-Dexia Investor Services as an architect-designer and Anu joined the Bank Santander (named Abbey National back then) as a customer advisor. I was young and ambitious, and the world was beautiful and full of possibilities.

Glorious Career

I worked very well in RBC-Dexia for a couple of years that landed me to the world's one of the most prestigious Investment Bank, JP Morgan Chase. My job profile was going to be even better than I had earlier dreamt during my MBA days. I was very happy and wanted to give my best shot in JP Morgan. At the same time, Anu continued to work in Santander till we decided to buy a house in Stanmore, a relatively peaceful and greener area in the North-West of Greater London. When we moved into our house, Anu fell pregnant with our son Zoravar Singh and he was born in early April 2008. I had got more than I had desired for. When I look back, that was the best time of my life till then and all my dreams were coming true.

I had impressed myself when I had positioned myself as Vice-President in JP Morgan and I hadn't even reached my mid-30s. I had worked incredibly hard to attain the position. Life was wonderful. My love deepened for my wife Anu and my son, Zoravar. During the weekdays, I would work hard and spend my weekends, literally photographing baby Zoravar or making countryside trips.

My parents back in India were proud of me and I was eagerly looking to the future. I still had lots of fire in my belly to do more and I had no doubt that with Anu with me, my desires will land me somewhere.

But alas that was just a fantasy! I had completely ignored the factors that were external to me and completely out of my control!

Financial Crisis of 2008

Nobody had anticipated the Financial Crisis of 2008, that were next only to the great economic meltdown of 1930's. Who can forget the collapse of Lehman Brother in mid-September of 2008; and the pictures that emerged of employees, leaving the building with their belongings? Those pictures were sending the chills down in everyone's spine, especially in the Financial Markets. Non-trading employees from departments such as Information Technology and Operations were extremely vulnerable and were sacked en masse. In spite of that however, JP Morgan had stood tall and had emerged as a survivor in the crisis, securing my future as well. Since I was responsible to roll out the VAT Infrastructure for the whole Group i.e., all its 'Lines of Businesses', my manager assured me that my career in the 'Tax' area is safe and secure and all we needed to do was to demonstrate the validity of our work to the regulators of the UK, especially HMRC (Her Majesty's Revenue and Customs). Thereafter, I just put my head down and kept pressing on to build the Tax infrastructure that HMRC eventually attested as 'State of Art Implementation' in the middle of year 2010.

Tough Times

Three years later in year 2011, mainstream media and general public had however, long forgotten the crisis of 2008; and they did not matter anymore to anyone outside the Financial World. But, within the financial world it was a completely different story. The impact of the crisis had reached at the floor levels. With this impact came extremely toxic working environment in the industry that permeated to all management levels. Realizing that soon I shall be dragged into this, I decided to make a safety net to avoid any embarrassing situation by initiating my own software development at home, the ideas that I had kept in the backburner till then. To do the coding, I would wake up at insane hours of 2:30 in the early morning and would typically spend over 3 hours till the dawn, and then travel to the office to make an early start to the day before 8:00 AM.

I continued with this trend that was only broken when my angelic daughter Nimrat Singh arrived in mid-November 2011. My pace of coding the software started to drop and my greed to spend more time with Zoravar and baby Nimrat started to soar. Eventually, I began to shelve my projects, unfortunately never to be picked again! But what I started to do instead was to start going to gym first thing in morning, waking up at 5AM every working day. By end of the day, I would feel tired and, on my way, back to home, I would typically listen to audio of motivational books. The words would keep me awake during the train journey after a long and tiresome day. I still had no regrets in life because I had got what I 'really' wanted and was enjoying my family.

An Ugly Turn

However, things at office had started to take its toll and the head of my department started to doubt the implementation and authenticity of the reports that were being automatically sent to HMRC. Me and my boss, and my VAT SME[3] colleague landed on one side of the argument and unfortunately the rest of the department was unconcerned beyond survival in this tough environment. Since all the work and the reports were duly attested by HMRC, I had full confidence in my work and in my integrity.

This covert environment continued all through the Christmas period turned out to be over whelming for me and had started to suffocate me. By the end of year 2012, I had started to suffer from stress and depression and ended up consulting my GP (General Practitioner). There was hardly any celebration for us at home that year. I felt terribly guilty that we could not celebrate much of Diwali and Christmas that year; particularly when they were meant to be Nimrat's first 'real' celebrations, as she was one year old by then.

---

[3]Subject Matter Expert

At the turn of the new year 2013, things had started to turn really nasty. This was a period of 'no' mercy; the friends were turning in foes and fights were being fought openly now; sackings for the sake of personal gains, under the garbs of 'disciplinary' actions, were a becoming a norm – all to satisfy the narcissist tendencies of senior managers.

Finally, things came to a head. The aftermaths of the havoc created by the Financial crisis reached my department as well when my boss, Chris, who gave 38 years of his loyal service to the bank, was sacked without much justification in middle of 2013. That single event turned out to be a big psychic set back to me as well and for some reason, I lost all the will to work. Once my boss was shown the doors so unceremoniously, I clearly saw that the monster of work politics will turn its ugly head towards me because I was second in responsibility of that particular domain i.e., submitting Bank's VAT to (and claiming the recovery from) HMRC.

That's exactly what happened a month after his departure. Where I had prepared myself to face any audit or investigation into my work, I saw no hope of rationality or fair play. I was not a 'manipulator' and foresaw a no-win situation for myself. When the crisis actually started to engulf me, I found myself caught up in covert threats. Ultimately, in order to protect my integrity and dignity, I resigned from my glorious career in the middle of August 2013, without securing a new job, because I knew that now Chris being gone, I'll end up attesting the 'incorrect' numbers of VAT liabilities and effectively betray HMRC - after having secured their goodwill just a few months earlier.

This was the last thing I had imagined could ever happen to my career. Of course, I could have stayed there and survived, but I would have had to go against my conscience, which I knew I would never do.

Hunt for Job

I was jobless in the in the market for first time ever in my life and had joined the 'employees with their belongings', that I had never envisioned to be. There were no jobs in the market, except the regulatory compliance ones; in wake of tough regulations that were being imposed on the

Financial Sector by all the governments across the world.

I must have attended around 10 interviews over the span of 6 weeks, but luck seemed to have abandoned me. I had started to give up and my stress factors were soaring. But somehow, I would manage to pull myself up and go for an interview. The torture lasted for 2 months and it was already October end, with yet one more Diwali that the family was going to let go without any. celebrations.

I was at the time of completely giving up, with a thought to move my young family back to India, when one day I received an interview call from Royal Bank of Scotland (RBS) in the heart of the city and from their global head office at Liverpool Street. I was in no mood of attending and just wanted to decline it. But Anu wasn't happy with my decision and challenged me:

"If you don't attend the interview, what are your chances of getting the job?"

"Zero Percent, of course" - I replied.

"And if you do go for the interview and just 'be yourself', how much chances do you see?".

"Given my recent negative experience, one to five percent"

"Still, isn't that number bigger than zero?"

The penny dropped. The keyword in this short conversation was "be yourself". I did not waste any time and straight went ahead for the interview and reported at the Bank's reception.

The manager in charge along with a senior Business Analyst interviewed me for an hour and I performed well. I had not even reached home, when I received a call from the recruiting desk making an offer for the role.

Finally, after over 2 months and over a dozen of interviews, I was made an offer as a freelancer 'Senior Business Analyst' in the UK's much troubled Bank.

The financial position of RBS was in a dire state when it

had become infamous as a 'troubled bank' and was rescued by the British government by injecting £45 billions of Taxpayer's money. I took the offer, but I knew working in this troubled institution was not going to be an easy sail at all!

I started my work in RBS in the middle of November 2013 and did managed to celebrate Diwali on November 3rd. Also, we made an overnight trip to Leicester Space Centre, to celebrate the occasion, as the Space Centre is Zoravar's favorite place to visit.

On day one itself, I was assigned on a 'mission critical' project in Banks' Operations division, where it was paramount to fix the broken processes of customer on-boarding and off-boarding across the globe. I had a rough start on the project because the processes were neither designed nor documented ever, which is not very unusual in old and big organizations. The state of data was worse than the reference data[4] that I had resolved 5 years ago at JPMorgan. This was primarily because the RBS had first

---

[4]Data that Banks and Organisations refer to process transactions such as data of the customers, daily stock market index value, daily currency exchange rates and many more.

expanded exponentially in Europe by acquiring some other big names such as ABN-AMRO, of Netherlands and then had a sudden collapse during the Financial Crisis of 2008. Because of sudden expansion and instant collapse, these investments had turned out to be 'very toxic' investments, wiping out all the wealth that the Bank had built, and RBS turned out to be one of the worst sufferers.

I started to work with the multi-stream teams across the global offices, wherever RBS or its subsidiaries had any presence; and my immediate challenge was to sort out the business process issues in the legacy ABN-AMRO processes, that had resulted in the bankruptcy of RBS. I started my job with just a dump of data that I was meant to reverse reengineer to understand the whole business process of customer on-boarding and off-boarding. When I looked at the data, it made absolutely no sense at all and I literally wanted to reject the work, but something inside me suggested to accept the challenge and turn things around. All I came to know that I had two predecessors on the job, and they had failed to make any progress, and had left the organization in disgust.

Further, this whole lack of understanding of data was making my manager and my colleagues very uncomfortable. I had started to feel very insecure, because I felt everyone was making mockery of my situation. My first reaction was that I had been assigned the riskiest job deliberately, but then I accepted it as a challenge and decided to give all I had to resolve the issue.

Soon I discovered that it wasn't anybody's fault either. The whole crisis of 2008 had brought extreme duress in the employees all over the job markets, that gave rise to mistrusts in office floors. What I thought was mockery, was nothing personal towards me but a phase, where nobody would trust a newcomer, and everyone was just protecting his/her job. I became even more determined to produce the results, because my survival was dependent on my performance alone.

Stress and Depression

I was performing well on my job but by being on non-stop mental roller coaster for almost a year and a half, my health had started to suffer; yet I kept ignoring it making my work as absolutely the first priority. The bank was under intense pressure to comply with newly imposed regulations in the wake of financial crisis and all the required compliance had a deadline by end of June 2015; and here I was struggling to even make the sense of completely convoluted processes and the data that had no head or tail anywhere. But I held a strong will and would often say to myself – "if anyone can get to the bottom of this fiasco, then it would be me". I just ignored my health and continued with my work, searching for light at an end of the dark and long tunnel.

I was pushing myself against the capacity of my body and my *brain*. I have always been a gym goer, but now I was finding it all impossible to do anything. All I could do was the analysis of the data 'dump', and the undocumented and completely wracked operational processes. With time, even traveling to the city was become a big burden for me. I have been seeing my GP since my struggle during winters of 2012 during my JP Morgan days. During approximately in a year and half, my GP's conclusion was that I have taken a hit of Financial Crisis and my *stresses* and *depression* was not unique to me, it was much prevalent in the city at that time and lots of people like me were bearing the brunt of the crisis.

Temporary Relief

However, in early January 2015, I began to have success at work and had started to make sense of all the legacy business processes just by analyzing the 'broken' databases. Once I started to share the results with my manager, stakeholders and colleagues, they felt relived as well and eventually I was allowed to give presentation to the compliance heads of my recommendations to mend the business processes and how to stay complaint for the regulations in the future. I congratulated myself on my success, on achieving the milestone that I had earlier set as my goal.

Two years later when I looked back, all I recalled that I have been pushing myself very hard indeed. I had no clue that I had started to take things very personally and had started to ignore my wellbeing and my health completely. Nevertheless, I had no regrets either, because *taking things personally*, was very important to get that particular job done at that time.

Symptoms

As I continued to accept the challenges that life was throwing at me, I was completely ignoring some early signals of ill-health that were going to hit me shortly:

- I had started to slow down, both physically and mentally. I have been a regular gym goer all my life and pretty good in software writing, yet all my previous strengths had unfortunately started to betray me now.
- I had started to suffer from Insomnia and sometimes would just sleep for 2 hours and make a very early start at work.
- My limbs had started to go numb while working on desk. Also, I had started to curl my fingers during the sleep.
- I was becoming lethargic day by day. Where I had a horse like stamina earlier, now I was developing into a sloth. I was losing my energy and had no will left to play with my children either.
- I wasn't romantic with Anu anymore and would often

lose my temper at her, irrationally, only to feel guilty later.

- I had started to get severe mood swings and I was turning into hypersensitive being at my work. Even constructive feedbacks from my colleagues, at work had started to threaten me.

- I had started to imagine illness, for example, when I got seasonal cold, my imagination was it to be revival of asthma I had briefly endured during my childhood.

In nutshell, my body and my *mind* had actually started to fail me, and I paid no attention to it. To me, the regular updates from the CEO of the Bank, Ross McEwan, had taken lot more importance than my health. The CEO used to be upbeat, always giving positive messages to the employees and the market, about the bright future that the bank has and how the colleagues who are working 'incredibly hard and intelligently' will restore the lost glory of the bank.

His messages would give me adrenaline rush, and I would work even harder. I pressed harder and harder and any thought or concern of my health completely vanished from my consciousness.

Soon my symptoms had start to exaggerate and I had started to show new and severe symptoms, that were going to panic me big time.

- I was developing *phobia of heights*, called vertigo, and would always avoid looking down from the higher floors of my office building.
- I had started to get dizzy spells in the lifts at my work. Once, as I stepped out of the lift, my colleague saw me getting dizzy and offered me coffee, at the café on the same floor.
- While traveling in London underground, I had started to hold the handles very firmly in the trains, and yet I would feel imbalanced whenever I would step out of the train.
- My lethargy had turned into extreme lethargy. I was increasingly finding it difficult to come out the bed in mornings and had started to get late to my work. Thankfully, I had built my good reputation by then.
- I had started to show forgetfulness that had started to

give concerns to Anu as well. For example, once I completely forgot that I had drove the car to the train station and yet in the evening I called Anu from the same station to pick me up.

- Another symptom was very short temper at work and at home. My threshold of patience had fallen to bare minimum. Fortunately, everyone kept forgiving me including my boss at work and Anu and my children at home.

- I had started to get hunger pangs and often they were uncontrollable. I had started to eat junk from the vending machines in the office, whereas I had always eaten healthy all my life.

- The only relief I used to get was when I would visit my barbers for haircuts every three weeks. Whenever the barber would touch my "scalp", it used to relax me immensely. On occasions when he would ask how my job is going, I would just reply – "Very stressful indeed – my only time of relaxation and calmness is on your chair"

Ironically, I still kept attributing these symptoms to the stress and depression, that I have carrying and contacted my GP for advice. I finally, in discussions with him, sought to seek psychotherapy session from some reputed therapist in the city.

Psychotherapy

I searched the internet and found a very impressive lady Psychotherapist, Joanne Renault, who ran her own counseling services specializing in stress and anxiety just a walking distance from Chalk Farm underground station, that lies on my way from office. After a couple of talks over the phone, I decided to seek therapy from her.

The first couple of sessions comprised all my catharsis of the terrible time I felt I had endured and after that Joanne, started to give me tips as how I could handle my stress levels and ways how I could bring more assertiveness in my body language. I began to improve my situation in office and began to be more assertive (yet considerate), in dealings in my office. I started to apply this formula in every dealing across all departments, and gradually I started to feel better.

Hardly 3 weeks had passed with Joanne, when in the early part of February 2105, I had started to feel that numbness in my limbs was getting worse, especially in left side. Soon I started to feel the numbness in the nights as well and it started to trouble me. I saw my GP again and got it checked. But by then we had started to attribute everything to continuously building stress and depression. I discussed the numbness with Joanne as well and we again concluded that these are the symptoms of extreme level of stress and depression. Extreme, because I have been carrying stress almost every day since the mid 2012 during my JPMorgan days, almost two and half years ago. I made a decision to focus on the therapy and not worry about these ailments for now.

In next few days as I talked more during my therapy sessions with Joanne and talks with Anu at home, I forgot the numbness altogether.

But that was unfortunately just a temporary phase and later it was going to come back and along with it were to come even bigger symptoms that were going to overshadow these ones.

Big Symptoms

Since I was suffering from insomnia too and the most logical justification was *stress* and *depression* (yet again), Joanne suggested me to take supplements of 'Melatonin' every night last thing before I go to sleep. I started to do that but there was a problem. Though Melatonin was working but it was working too much. I would take it in night before going to bed and just wouldn't get up in the mornings. It was like an extreme hangover one gets after a drinking bout a night before.

The morning sloppiness had gone worse. But I told myself, that curing stress and depression is more important than anything else right now and gave therapy the top priority. By mid-March 2015, I had started to ignore even my GP.

But in the therapy also, things were not perfect, and I had started to falter. My *retention power* of Joanne's advices had started to get very short, and she had to repeat the same tips over and over again. The psychotherapy was giving results initially, but shortly they too turned out to be ineffective. But I was keeping my hopes alive and did not want to stop the therapy. Whereas I would meet Joanna with brave face, but in my mind, I have been harboring some deep fears, that I was too scared to reason with myself or share with anyone else.

By mid 2015, my condition was getting worst and I had started to show some severe and embarrassing symptoms.

- I had started to collapse without any forewarning reactions in body. This happened twice in my office. On first occasion, I fell on the main road while crossing the traffic lights just outside my office building and thankfully the traffic had stopped on the red light. The security guards saw me collapsing and brought me into the office lounge. My boss, called the taxi and sent me to the nearby hospital for checkup, that again revealed nothing. On the second occasion, I had collapsed outside the washroom in the office, and since no one saw me falling, I did not make any issue either and just continued to work with my head down as if nothing had happened.
- I had started to suffer from urine incontinence and

bowel incontinence. I felt too awkward and embarrassed to mention this to my GP and even Anu and Joanne, and foolishly, I had started to device my own methods to prevent this. To avoid urine urgency, I had started to empty my bladder every time I would step out of office or home. To prevent the bowel urgency, I had started to consume absolutely dry meals and often I would just consume plain baguettes in lunch. Moreover, I would always assure that I am in proximity of toilets whenever I go out of home or office. Managing this lifestyle wasn't an easy job at all, but somehow, I did drag myself to do it.

I discussed all my symptoms with Dr Gould (except incontinence) and Dr Gould's advice was to perform a 'complete blood culture' to ensure there is nothing infectious in my blood. Due to lack of facilities in the surgery, the blood culture was booked in a medical centre some 4 miles north of my home and a mile from the underground train station of Rayners Lane.

The Big Collapse

On 29th September 2015, I left my work just after the lunch to reach Rayners Lane in time for the appointment. Anu had earlier suggested that she would pick me from the station and drive me to the medical centre. From the station, when I called her, she was waiting across the road. I couldn't spot her, but she saw me coming out from the station and told me to cross the pedestrian crossing and reach the car.

I kept coming out from the station on a steep slope and started to walk bit faster in the crowd. Suddenly, I did not notice and hit a lamp post. Before I could realize, I began to run down the slope. I must have been very fast because Anu too had lost the sight of me in the crowd. Nevertheless, before I was to run berserk on the main road, I had managed to turn into the street and was literally sprinting inside the street and found very difficult to control myself. Eventually, when the slope ended, I fell very badly on the kerbside. My suit was badly torn. My body was all rattled and injured with cuts and bruises.

In the meantime, Anu was searching for me frantically and trying to call me on my mobile. Just seconds ago, she had an eye on me and was talking to me, and yet I had now disappeared and there was no trace of me. She got concerned and took a risk of leaving the car at the side of the main road and came out of it to search for me.

I was lying on the kerbside with no sense of where I was. People gathered around me. Moments later, Anu saw this crowd around me and ran into the street. She was horrified to see me collapsed and dazed. When I saw her, I got some grip on myself. She called the emergency services. Moments later, when I could collect myself, I explained everything to her. First, she made sure I am not badly hurt and then called the clinic, we here heading to. A kind resident where I fell, offered me water that calmed me down. Few minutes later, a paramedic arrived and took the blood sample on the spot. Some more tests that she performed concluded that everything was fine with my body. The paramedic advised us to go to the hospital for further check-ups related to the heart. Anu drove me to the A&E of the Northwick Park Hospital that lies closer to our house.

At the A&E, I was checked by a team of doctors. The

team saw the blood report that the paramedic gave to me earlier and inquired about my symptoms. When I narrated them, they investigated about my past medical history, especially of any heart conditions that could be running in my family. There was nothing of that sort that ran in my family. After the interrogation, I stated that my blood tests and heart condition is absolutely fine, but I need to get my head checked. I complained that I always feel as if the *brain is being compressed from inside*. This was the first time ever I had made a reference to my *brain*.

The team leader inquired bit more about my symptoms and discharged me a little later instructing that I need to co-ordinate further through my GP, and in the meantime, she would forward her notes to my surgery.

We came home but I was still confused what could be wrong with me. I hurriedly searched the internet about the symptoms and found it could be blood clot in the brain that is causing all this. I also found that with 'blood thinners', the clots in 'early' stages could be dissolved without much side impact on patient's health, using simple medicines such as aspirin and/or warfarin. With this wishful thinking especially with the 'early' stage clause, I gave myself some relief. But I still wanted to talk to my GP about this theory of blood clots.

When I narrated the episode of my fall to my GP, he heard everything patiently but did not pay any attention to my claims of blood clots. After I had completed my story, his remarks were "I would now like to get to the real bottom of this whole thing by sending you for an MRI scan".

He however, still prescribed anti-depressants to me and advised complete rest till I have relaxed fully and on the same night I notified my boss that I'll be away from work for few weeks for thorough checkups. I realized that I could lose my assignment, but in that moment I did not care. I was finally awakened to the state of my health and personal care all of a sudden had become the first priority for me.

A couple of days later, I received a letter conforming the MRI scan on November 10, 2015. I felt disappointed that the scan date was six weeks away and it did not seem an urgent issue to the scanning centre. I called the scan centre and they explained that the earliest date they could offer to me. I had no option but to accept the date. I decided to take rest along with the anti-depressants as it seemed that it was all stress related and decided to return to work only when I feel fully relaxed and recovered. My manager was fine with the arrangement and assured me that he will keep an opening for me and wished me good luck to recover soon.

Diagnosis and Treatment

Tough times never last, but tough people do.

- Robert H. Schuller

I was on rest and October had started. On the morning of 1st October, I received a phone call from my cousin in Chandigarh, my birthplace and hometown in India. He was getting married on 25th October, i.e., 25 days later. He mentioned that he would feel nice if we all could come over. I thought for a while and concluded that going for a week or so won't do any harm and I should get relief from the misery and stress I had been enduring for almost three years. I just needed a change for few days to calm myself down, something that could distract me from the depressing time I had been having.

I shared my thoughts with Anu and stressed I needed a break. Incidentally, the wedding coincided with children's half term at school as well. I was on prescribed anti-depressants and to my mind, suffering from stress should alleviate during these few days.

Trip to India

I booked the flight for October 24th and returning a week later on November 1st. I felt immense relief already and started to look forward to the trip.

We reached Chandigarh in the afternoon of October 24th, 2015 a day before the wedding. The next day on the wedding, we reached the venue on time where I met with my sister, Dr Rupinder Sangha and my brother-in-law, Dr JPS Sangha. They are successful doctors and run their own hospital in a city called Ropar, just 20 miles north of Chandigarh. They were keen to inquire about the symptoms I had in London, but due to the busy ceremony, nothing could be discussed.

The following day, sister and Dr Sangha came over to my parents' house and we continued with our discussions regarding the symptoms. I put forward the same 'blood clot' theory to them and it was rejected yet again. I requested them to keep me in their hospital for few days and perform some tests to establish what exactly could be wrong with me. My brother-in-law and sister welcomed me to stay in the hospital, but advised that before we leave for Ropar, we must get an *MRI Scan* done at the city's leading diagnostic centre, Atulaya.

The Scan

The next morning, Dr Sangha took me to the scan centre. My father accompanied us while sister stayed back at home with my mother. Anu and kids had gone to her parent's house straight after the wedding and they were still there.

A lengthy MRI scan was performed on me for over 40 minutes and stopping halfway to inject a 'contrasting agent' in my body so that the radiologist could see more clearly if there is any abnormal activity in my brain. When I came out of the scan, I was suffering from usual hunger pangs and by the time I finished eating the sandwich, Dr Sangha had already started the discussions with the radiologist.

When the discussions were over, he came out of the meeting room to the lobby and said to father - "I am afraid, it's the worst-case scenario that we had anticipated" and then looking at me "It's a growth, possibly a Glioma".

I had gone completely baffled when he mentioned these words to me and had not registered them at all. In complete disbelief, I could only utter "Sorry?" … urging him to repeat his words. He repeated the same thing again, gently and giving vibes of comfort to me and father. I still could not believe what Dr Sangha was saying because that was a big C word that I had never imagined could ever happen to me, and that too in my brain! The Earth seemed to slip from under my feet. Life had jolted me with the biggest shock it could give. I had gone completely stunned for a few moments. I was breathing very heavily in fear and extreme anxiety.

Dr Sangha interrupted for good – "Let's get out of here and collect ourselves at home".

It took around 30 minutes to reach home, but those 30 minutes were not passing and seemed 30 millenniums to me. I was sinking in fear and anxiety sitting in rear seat of the car. When we reached home, mother and sister opened the door of the lounge and the news was revealed to them. Surprisingly, my mother looked extremely collected, which was contrary to her sensitive nature, as if she too had considered the 'worst case scenario'. Sister was collected too, but I could imagine that being a doctor, she was taking the news objectively. After taking few sips of water, I requested sister to call Anu because I needed her next to me at that time of personal crisis.

Sister did not disclose too much over the phone to Anu except that the "scan doesn't look very good". But, Anu arrived just after few minutes, leaving the kids at her parents'. We just hugged each other and sat together on the couch, and quietly re-establishing the strong bond we had always shared. With Anu next to me, my fear had started to abate a bit, and I held her hand.

Following the discussion over the MRI Scan, sister suggested the next step was to find a best hospital and the best neurosurgeon ASAP to perform the surgery on my brain to take the tumour out (called Craniotomy). Dr

Sangha made few calls and after an hour or so came up with a name of very reputed Neurosurgeon, Dr VK Khosla, who had earlier served as a head of Neurosurgery Department of Chandigarh's own premier Government Institute, PGI[5]. After retiring from PGI he has been serving in very reputed private hospital, Fortis, just few miles from my parents' house[6].

Sister had secured an earliest available appointment with Dr Khosla that was for the next evening i.e., October 28[th,] 2015. When we met with him, Dr Khosla asked me about my symptoms. I revealed everything including my incontinence episodes. I wasn't embarrassed anymore because now it was out that I was seriously ill. True to what was expected from him, he advised me to get admitted the following day so that I could be operated upon. That night, Dr Sangha and sister kept me on intravenous drip of steroids to prevent any potential stroke.

---

[5]Smaller abbreviation for PGIMR (Post Graduate Institute for Medical Research)

[6]Chandigarh is a modern, very planned city and all roads are straight, with a grid like architecture. With decent traffic discipline, the commute time is in minutes and never in hours.

Craniotomy

The next day, I was admitted in the hospital. Dr Khosla saw me in the ward and informed that he will operate on me the following morning at 6:30AM.

The rest of the evening went in preparation for the operation. Late in the evening, my head was shaven clean. Only Anu was allowed to stay with me in the ward and rest of our families had to either go home or stay in the lounge. I was given some sleeping pills immediately after an early dinner. Guess, I had to be switched off for my own benefit so that I don't indulge into any fearful thoughts at night. Anu spent the entire night sitting on couch at my bedside as I slept.

I was woken up by nurse at 5AM in the following morning on 30th October 2015. I was helped to a shower and my head washed with an antiseptic fluid by an attendent. By 6AM, I was ready to go to the Operation Theatre (OT).

I was taken to the OT on stretcher, where the anaesthesia team met me first. Before starting the surgery, they asked me few questions, mainly to check my mental faculties before the operation and started to dose me with the general anaesthesia. My last very vague recollection before the surgery is of anaesthesia team jolted me to check my consciousness that I was losing rapidly.

When I opened my eyes, I found myself in the ICU (Intensive Care Unit) and Anu beside my bed. I felt no energy to move and could only look at her. She sat on the chair next to my bed. We did not talk at all and she was just looking at me and my surgery with the most tender eyes. She touched my arm gently and from eyes I gave my response. After few minutes, when she had quietly gauged that I looked OK, she left the ICU to inform the families.

I could not speak due to sores in my throat that were given by the anaesthesia tube. I could only give little smiles to greet staff around me. Since I was drugged extensively, I had no clue of day or night either. I was injected with pain killers and sleeping drugs to keep me in slumber all the time.

When I woke up next, I could look at the clock straight ahead. It was morning - 10AM of November 1st, the days we were meant to catch our return flight. By then, I was feeling bit better; the nurse came around me to give me an oral pain killer for my throat. The nurse also informed me that in the afternoon, my surgeon, Dr Khosla would be visiting me, in the ICU.

Dr Khosla arrived just after 3PM and Anu was again sitting next to me. By that time, I had started to whisper. I could answer questions in one word. Dr Khosla mainly wanted to check my faculties and asked me some basic questions like my name, where I live, my wife's name and my children's names etc. I whispered all of them correctly and he left me assuring that I just need recovery.

In the morning of November 2nd, I had recovered a little bit more and around noon time, I was shifted to a private room. On the way to the private room, in the corridor, my mother, sister, father, brother and my father-in-law waved at me. I smiled at everyone and they were all assured that I am well.

I stayed in the private room for 6 nights, then I was discharged to go home. During these days, it was discovered that my left side was completely paralysed. The physiotherapy team checked me, and they found that my body was responding to the sensations of 'touch' though. They confirmed that the paralysis is only temporary and with massage and physiotherapy, it would be restored.

The physiotherapist had started to come at home in the morning time. I had a couple of caregivers as well dedicated to me for 24 hours.

With physiotherapy, I had started to make good progress and within a week I was on my feet, albeit with a walking frame. A few days later I had started to gently move of my own, without any aid, and that impressed everyone, and my speedy recovery was attributed to the strong body and equally *strong will power* I had held throughout.

During these days, Anu acted as my nurse and she would take care of my medicines and dose at prescribed times. I would always feel calm in her presence.

Once I had started to take steps, mother stepped in to restore my physique. She loved giving me pressed mosambi (sweet lemon) juice multiple times a day along with fresh fruit salad. My friends would bring fresh coconuts for me daily and I would drink water from them.

I was making good progress and had started to go on slow walks in a park opposite to the house in the evenings. Initially someone would assist me in walking but soon I was walking alone, albeit very slowly.

On November 27th, 20 days after my discharge, it was my birthday. I felt like celebrating and requested my brother, Aman, to arrange a dinner party for my side of family and Anu's side of the family in a fine curry house and he did so. I enjoyed the dinner, and the highlight was my sister-in-law, Mona, who flew all the way from California to meet me when she heard about my illness.

After a day or so, I expressed my desire to sister and Dr Sangha that I would like to get the further treatment through NHS in London and would like to stay at my comfort zone, my own little castle i.e., my home. They agreed to my proposal and being doctors themselves, they knew that NHS would provide a world class treatment for this critical condition. We went to Fortis to get travel approval. In the absence of Dr Khosla, his deputy conducted my review, did some cognitive checks and issued a 'fit to fly' statement.

We landed in London on the night of Thursday, December 9th, 2015, almost five weeks later than our planned return date. Anu's best friend in the UK and work colleague along with her husband picked us from the airport, took us to our home and laid me in my bed.

Radio-Chemotherapy

While I was on bed in India, Anu had kept my GP and Joanne, my psychotherapist, along with my colleagues at RBS and JP Morgan informed about my diagnosis and the surgery. The next morning after we landed, Anu called the surgery to book an appointment with my GP, Dr Lawrence Gould. She secured an appointment for Monday, 14th December.

During the appointment I was informed by Dr Gould that I have already been referred to UCLH (University College London Hospital). A very talented and esteemed Oncologist, Dr Jeremy Rees, would be my consultant. He further stated that from here onwards, he and his surgery will only keep a watch of my overall wellbeing during the treatment and provide me with essential support as and when needed. I was wished good luck for the treatment.

The next day, we contacted UCLH and found out that being a Christmas period, Dr Rees is on holiday and shall resume his duties after Christmas and New Year on January 6th. I had no option but to wait till Dr Rees was back.

On 4th January 2016, we called UCLH again to secure an appointment with Dr Rees on or around 6th January itself. But I was taken aback when we were told that during the Christmas holidays, Dr Rees had caught viral infection and will be out of work for another one week. My appointment was booked for January 13th instead. But in order to move things forward, we were told to drop the sample of the tumour earliest possible so that the pathology on the sample could be performed before Dr Rees resumes his work. The next morning, Anu went to UCLH and handed over the sample[7], we had brought from India. Because of my condition, I was unable to travel on the underground trains, hence Anu drove me to the hospital in the centre of the city.

My mother-in-law had arrived on the Christmas eve to support us on the. She was quick to take the affairs of the kitchen and started to look after my diet immediately. During her stay, she was going to feed me with lots of garlic, ginger and turmeric. Her argument was that these root ingredients are full of antioxidants and have anti-inflammatory properties and will assist in healing the tumour. Henceforth, diet and nutrition started playing an important part in my daily regimen (and it continue to be so at the time of writing this text in mid-2021).

Then 13th Jan came, and it was a day to finally meet Dr Rees.

---

[7]Sister had warned us that NHS would be asking for the Tumour sample to perform their own biopsy. She had sent the sample with us.

At the meeting, the first thing Dr Rees asked me was – "What is your understanding of the Tumour you have?". I thought Dr Rees is checking my faculties and I answered what was told to me by the Fortis hospital back in India.

"I have Grade 2 Oligodendroglioma".

"I am afraid that is not the case as per the latest biopsy results, we have received from our labs" – he said.

That comment confused me all of a sudden and I could not figure out what Dr Rees could mean. My first reaction was to doubt the biopsy of the tumour performed by Fortis.

With deep and sinking breath I asked, "What does the latest biopsy tell us Doctor".

"As per the report, it is Grade 4 Glioblastoma - or GBM for short".

"But Dr Rees, it is supposed to be Grade 2 and not Grade 4"

"Unfortunately, that is the nature of the brain tumours. Different slices of the tumour give different grading of the Tumour. Grade 4 is worst, but with that knowledge you couldn't possibly get under treated"

I accepted the argument but was not prepared to hear that word – GBM. Based on Grade 2 Tumour, I had projected my life span of up to another few years or so and GBM primarily implies lifespan not in years but in months and I would have to be "extremely" lucky to survive in years span. I sank completely and had never had that feeling before. It was even worse than the feelings I had when I had come to know in Chandigarh's diagnostic centre that I had Brain Cancer.

Moment later, I somehow collected my breath and my question with deep sigh to Dr Rees was an obvious one:

"Doctor, how must time do you think I have?"

"The way you have travelled to my clinic and the way you are standing; I don't want to put any number on you".

That assured me a little, but I was still very anxious and far from relieved.

Dr Rees asked me to walk in his room so that he could assess my gait[8]. I showed my gait, and it was alright. I asked Dr Rees about my performance. He said, "You have to do lot worse than that to convince me that you are not in physically good state". I felt the first spark of assurance and for the first time I smiled in the meeting.

Dr Rees remarked further: You are otherwise a healthy and strong man and I can give you a very high 'Karnofsky performance score' (KPS). That was another new term for me, but the way Dr Rees had put it, I gathered that if he is complementing me for a 'high' score, then this high must mean something good, unlike the 'high grade' of the tumour.

By then, I had recovered from the initial shock of the conversation and blatantly questioned . "Doctor, what would be next step in my treatment?"

---

[8]The way a person/patient walk.

Dr Rees mentioned that he is convinced that we could begin with Radio-Chemotherapy as soon as possible. The protocol that he stated was that I will undergo 6 weeks of radiotherapy and in parallel, I will get 'incremental' doses of chemotherapy as well[9].

The meeting with Dr Rees ended and we were on our way out.

On the exit, I noticed that Anu's mood was sombre, a rare side of her I have had never seen, from otherwise such a strong woman. After coming out of the hospital, she finally revealed her fears. Having done some research she was extremely scared of aggressive nature of the tumour (GBM) that Dr Rees had just mentioned:

"I don't want to lose you. You are the only man I want to have in my life" – she said. I immediately adored her and convinced her - "Anu, don't worry. We are where we are, and it is what it is. I promise to you that I will give all I have in me to overcome this disease". I had always taken

---

[9]Sometimes chemotherapy is given alongside the radiotherapy to make the treatment more effective.

81

her strength for granted and had never realized that she too is a human with feelings, emotions and love for her family. Moreover, she looked exhausted. Though, with my remarks, she looked a bit reassured.

It was past lunch time, and we were hungry. We went to the nearby pub and ate their 'homemade' sandwiches along with tea. By the time we finished our lunch, we had talked through the GBM news that we had just heard. We vowed to give our best shot and never falter no matter how much the treatment knocks me down. We reached home in the evening after 5PM and after a little relaxation, I went to peaceful sleep. In the morning, we called our families in India and gave a briefing of our meeting with Dr Rees. Everyone was non-reactive to the news, perhaps they were prepared to hear the 'high grade' word. But I was wished good luck and my parents and Anu's father gave their blessing.

I did not wish to travel 'into' the city on the underground and I had let this known to Dr Rees during out meeting earlier. That's the reason Dr Rees was going to book me at MVCC (Mount Vernon Cancer Centre), which was an extension of UCLH in the outskirts of greater London, 12 miles further out from my home in Stanmore, and had the same radiation and scanning facilities as UCLH in the city centre. The oncologists and other senior medical staff, including Dr Rees, split their week in UCLH and MVCC.

The next stage was to wait for the radio-chemotherapy call, patiently at home. To spend time, and to keep myself distracted from the fearful thoughts, I decided to understand more about my illness on the internet.

While browsing the net, I came across the statistics published by various agencies. They all gave grim picture of survival such as this curve below from Neuro-Oncology of University of California at Los Angeles (UCLA).

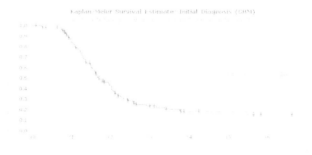

Fig 1: Estimated survival time of GBM patients. Source- UCLA

I studied the curve closely and observed that half of the GBM patients were dying within 633.5 days or just under 2 years, called the median survival rate. It was a scary picture indeed. Then I took a closer look at the curve again and concentrated on the bottom half of the curve. I observed that the other half of the GBM patients were actually living 'beyond' 2 years. On much closer look, towards the right, it was apparent that there is a tiny minority that continue to live beyond 6 years as well and since the curve had no end that implied that there must be at least a very small fraction of patients that must be surviving for long term. That gave me an idea I wanted to explore.

I decided that I could try to 'scurry' into that very narrow side of the curve at the bottom, the tunnel with no end, and shall do my best to penetrate as far as possible. That gave me immense motivation and changed my perception of things completely. I did not know for how long I was going to survive, but my spirit soared all of a sudden and I concluded that I need to stay absolutely calm and need to act like a 'peaceful warrior' to put a good fight against this beast of GBM. From that day onwards, I never felt any fear of death (for a long time).

While I was trying to digest some more GBM material on the internet, I received a letter from Prof Peter Hoskins, radiotherapy oncologist, at MVCC Hospital. Since we were going to drive outside the city and not inside, I and Anu concluded that it would make a pleasant drive for us.

We met with Prof Hoskins in the end of Jan 2016. Prof Hoskins knew almost everything about my case. A specialist nurse was also assigned to me and her name was Maggie Fitzgerald, who later turned out to be very caring and intelligent person during my treatment and would continue to be my nurse for next two years, till she got promoted to the head nurse of Oncology department of MVCC and equally caring head nurse, Tanya Betts was appointed instead on my case.

Prof. Hoskins laid down a protocol of 'radio-chemotherapy' that was going to last for 6 weeks. The chemotherapy drug that was prescribed with radiotherapy was called 'Temozolomide' (TMZ in short). I was warned of the side effects of radiations such as hair loss and nausea and also, I was briefed on the side 'effects' of chemo drug TMZ, which included nausea, skin damage, constipation and decline in sexual appetite etc.

My radio-chemotherapy began in the early February 2016. Anu would drive me to get radiation every working day. By that time, my father-in-law, a retired and decorated Brigadier from the Indian army, had arrived and had started to accompany us to the radiotherapy session and boosting my morale all the time by telling various war tales of his courage to defend the country.

The first couple of weeks went well and I was surprised that none of the side effects were showing any signs. But things changed drastically during week 3 when within 2 days, I would pick hand full of hair from my head during shower. I had gone completely bald, even though it did not surprise me too much because I had been warned.

Surprisingly, I showed no other signs of negative effects of chemo drug, TMZ, not even nausea. Later, I was told that I was being given the drug in a moderate quantity to prepare the body for 'real onslaught' of the chemotherapy that was due to start after the radio-chemotherapy. I was scared - Is the 'real onslaught' yet to come?

The radiations finally ended after six weeks as planned. A few days later, I met with Dr Rees and he mentioned to me that for my further treatment of chemotherapy, I'll be under the care of very reputed oncologist Dr Paul Mulholland. After the meeting, Maggie assured me that "With Dr Mulholland I can receive the best care and he works very closely with Dr Rees. He also runs his own clinical trials and was closely related to many other trials and senior oncologists worldwide."

Chemotherapy TMZ

I met with Dr Paul Mulholland on Thursday, 7th April 2016 at MVCC. Just like Prof Hoskins, Dr Mulholland was also well conversant with my case.

After this meeting that ran for approximately 45 minutes, Dr Mulholland decided to give me prescription of '6 cycles of adjuvant Temozolomide chemotherapy'. Each cycle was to last for 28 days (4 weeks) and in each cycle the dose of TMZ was to be increased.

Dr Mulholland warned me of the side effects such as nausea and had prescribed anti sickness tablets that I was supposed to take an hour before the main TMZ drug. I foolishly ignored these warnings (in particular of the anti-sickness tablets) and felt that they won't do too much damage because I came out unscathed during the radio-chemotherapy with relative few side effects. I had completely forgotten that the new chemo dosage was going to be high and a 'real onslaught' on my body.

Further, I was not allowed to eat anything for 2 hours on either side of taking TMZ dose. That implied, I just had to have early dinner, take TMZ couple of hours later and straight go to sleep after that.

Unfortunately, once I started to take the dose, that was not easy at all. I would crunch my stomach trying to go to sleep in vain and the nausea and on top of that. I also had hunger pangs that brought on more sleeplessness. In the early days, I wouldn't sleep at all in the nights. But later, I started to wake up after midnight and Anu would give me dry toasts of wholemeal bread along with detoxifying herbal tea.

Cycle 1 of TMZ was still more or less uneventful, but my body had started to take a real hit from Cycle 2. Usually I could 'somehow' manage myself through the night. But for some reason nausea had it peaks in the early hours of morning around 4:00AM. I had started to vomit a lot. I had placed myself in a separate room downstairs, since we had come back from India in December 2015, as it had on-suite bathroom, and would sleep alone. Often, in those early hours, when I would feel nauseated Anu would rush downstairs to be with me. After every episode, I would wash my face and mouth, brush my teeth and endure the discomfort, and after the vomit had flushed the poison from my body, I would drift off to sleep. During my sleep, Anu would usually clean up the mess and ensuring me till I felt better again. That made me terribly guilty of putting her through so much trouble, as I was sure she had very little sleep herself and yet at the same time I was immensely grateful to have her as my caregiver. After my little naps, Anu would often give me SOS anti-nausea drug and a little later, a dry toast again with herbal tea. I would consume the toast and tea very slowly and it would generally take me almost up to an hour to finish this simple meal. But after completing it, I would feel somewhat recovered and energetic.

Overall, I had started to drop my weight, which was alarming. But that was not unexpected either because after all I had the most beastly disease in the world with big "C".

I had completely lost the will to read any motivational stuff. After making recovery in couple of days, I would watch documentary DVDs (Muhammad Ali's were a constant source), Rocky volumes or read few lines from some books (such as Bruce Lee's beautiful book – 'The Warrior Within'). They would pep me up for the next cycle of the treatment and closer to my next appointment date, I would even start walking in the nearby park to get some fresh air.

But, with the cycles of TMZ, my cycle of collapsing, getting up and moving again were extremely tiring and frustrating and I found it very difficult to keep my spirit up all the time. Yet, I would always remember some quotes which in their simplicity affected me:

"Keep moving forward. That's how winning is done" – Rocky Balboa.

"I hated every minute of training, but I said, 'Don't quit. Suffer now and live the rest of your life as a champion.'" – Muhammad Ali

And of course, this one from my 7-year-old son, Zoravar: "Sometimes bad things are nothing but good things in disguise."

I would listen to simple yet very serene Indian classical and instrumental music from the maestros such as Santoor from Pundit Shiv Kumar and Sitar from Pundit Ravi Shankar. The music would calm me down immensely.

At times, when I used to feel better, I loved spending time with my family. They gave me immense peace and love. All these activities kept me going in spite of all the trouble I had with the chemotherapy drugs.

Chemotherapy PCV

In the last week of June (just in the middle of cycle 3), one day Anu noticed that I am weak on my left leg and do not place my left foot firmly on the floor while standing or walking. She immediately informed the hospital by writing an email to Maggie.

Maggie further consulted Dr Mulholland and after a couple of hours conveyed to Anu that they would like to conduct an MRI scan of my head. I was called in for scan on July 14th, 2016.

After the scan, Dr Mulholland informed me that the TMZ drug has not been responding and the tumour is actually not showing any signs of remission. This was very upsetting. My instinct was that since we are just halfway in the treatment, there won't be any signs of recovery anyway. But I went with Dr Mulholland's observation that we have not been looking for recovery per se, but there were no 'noticeable signs' of positive effects of TMZ drug.

I was called again the following Thursday to Dr Mulholland's clinic. Dr Mulholland was now recommending an alternate treatment that was not a gold standard per se but was well researched and highly respected by the oncologists around the globe. The new drug was known as PCV, which essentially is a cocktail of three chemo drugs, and it stands for P - Procarbazine, C – Lomustine (also called CCNU[10]) and V - Vincristine. The 'cocktail' was to be given in cycles of 4 weeks each that included an intake of drugs for a week and followed by a rest or 'recovery' period for 3 weeks. Naively, I gently challenged Dr Mulholland that if the TMZ, the gold standard, did not work on me, on what basis we are assuming that PCV will work? Dr Mulholland, as usual very confidently replied that brain cancer is a very 'strange' disease, and it works differently for every person. He further asserted that when PCV works, it works very well and he has actually witnessed a number of positive results, where TMZ proved to be ineffective and PCV came to the rescue.

---

[10]CCNU- Named after the chemical formula of the drug; 1-(2-Chloroethyl)-3-Cyclohexyl-1-Nitrosourea.

The protocol was such that on day one of each cycle, I would get Vincristine, intravenously, straight after Dr Mulholland's prescription. The hospital had this facility where I would just walk into the chemotherapy suite at the prescribed time, where they would prepare the drug fresh and then inject into my body intravenously. I was informed that if the drug is not given to the patient within 2-3 hours, then the efficacy of the whole preparation goes away, and it goes stale.

Initially, the intravenous was not an issue, as I had fairly prominent veins due to the gym I had done in past, but with time the chemotherapy drug started to take toll on my body as my veins began to collapse. On one occasion to prepare me for the drip, the nurse had to actually dip my arms in warm water, till she could see the veins protruding from my skin.

Vincristine was just one drug in the cocktail that comprised two other drugs. The pharmacy within MVCC, would prepare the other drugs while Vincristine was being administered into my body. Procarbazine had to be taken as one dosage on the night 1 of the treatment, that comprised of 5 capsules. On top of that there was a 'primary' drug of the cocktail, Lomustine that I had to take from night 1 to all the way to night 7, four capsules per night. Even though I was warned that these drugs give a typical side effect of nausea, but I had grossly underestimated the extent to which I was going to suffer from them. From 1st night only, I struggled to take the medicines and would typically throw up. I had stopped everyone from coming into my room. But during these episodes, as always, Anu would stay by my side for comfort. Overall, the impact on the body was bigger than TMZ. In spite of taking the anti-nausea drugs, I was suffering very badly.

I was losing weight drastically and felt awfully weak. From a well-muscled 87 kilos I was shrinking fast, and my weight was dropping at a very alarming rate and eventually was soon to touch 69kilos (just under 11 stones). But I decided to keep going on and somehow would stretch myself for another 7 days of the cycle. In spite of all challenges, I finally decided to bear with everything because I knew that my strength was not over yet and whenever the scans happen again, it would reveal everything anyway. I was very clear that nothing is going to happen to me at least till the next scan that was due in 6 months or so.

Another reason that I continued with the treatment was that I knew if I make any more noise again, my treatment could be cut short and I would find myself under the MRI scanner again! I also endured the treatment because I had never stopped doing my normal day to day activities such as taking warm shower every day to keep myself hygienic and fresh.

I had no diet during those seven days. Nothing would suit me at all, no conventional vegetables, no fruit and not any of the dairy products. The only vegetables that suited me during those days were bitter, mustard greens and spinach soup; that too if I chew my food very slowly and in very small bites. Eating had become my full-time affair. The whole week used to be an extreme torture physically, mentally and morally. Only during the so called 'recovery period' of 3 weeks, I would feel marginally better to go for short walks in the nearby park or do some reading.

By the end of November, I had somehow managed to complete 4 cycles of the PVC chemo when I had also completely come off the anti-inflammatory steroids, Dexamethasone, that I have been taking since my craniotomy in India, in Oct' 2015, just more than a year ago. I had started to count down the days, as there were only two more cycles to go.

Alas my wishful thinking was short lived!

With the change of season from autumn to winters, the annual 'seasonal viral' also made a comeback. Usually, it gives flu and cold for few days and patient would recover to normalcy after that. Because of my low immunity, I took a bad case of the flu just before the Christmas of 2016. The flu brought with it lots of cough as well and I would think it would disappear within in few days. But it didn't and my new chemotherapy date of December 29th, 2016 was approaching fast. When there was no sign of relief, I contacted my GP and went to the surgery for check-up. What I thought was a simple case of seasonal viral turned out to be a chest infection. As if the chemo drugs were not enough, I had to take a strong dosage of antibiotics for one week .

The course of antibiotics brought the new lowest point in the whole treatment. I knew I had no option but to take this anti-biotic prescription and fix myself before getting chemo dose. That depressed me a lot as I hit the lowest levels of my physical and mental strength ever, which in turn brought extreme pessimism and fears of imminent death in me. My weight had hit an all-time low at 65 kilos (10.2 stones). It was like death was staring at me and I began to have real concerns for my young family should I just vanish from this world.

I struggled a lot with anti-biotic and its side effects of diarrhoea. I had started to lay on the bed all day and night. I had no strength to get up and move; leave alone going for my daily walks.

Finally, I had some relief by the appointment date of December 29th for planned cycle 5 of the chemotherapy and I dragged myself to the appointment and as always first went straight for my blood tests. But I felt so listless that I had no energy to expect for any positive blood test results.

When I met with Dr Mulholland and Maggie a couple of hours later, my fears were confirmed. I was told that I won't be getting my chemo drugs for the cycle and the primary reason was my blood tests revealed that my platelet[11] counts are very low at 38K per microlitre of blood, when the normal range is between 140K-400K per microlitre of blood. My neutrophil[12] count was also low at 1.5 (1500 / mm3 of blood) when they should be in the range of 1.8 to 7.7 (1800 to 7700 / mm3 of blood). But low platelet count was the main culprit. It was a panic moment and I felt very upset when Dr Mulholland said we have to wait till the count of both the deficiencies recover to the normal level. With sympathy, Maggie stated - "your body is already taking so many toxins and on top of that more antibiotics were not going to do any good to your health". Just then Dr Mulholland assured me that I need not worry as these counts have tendency to bounce back

---

[11]Platelets cells - vital component of blood, responsible to heal the wound.
[12]Neutrophil – while blood cells; essential for body's immunity.

quickly within days, conditionally I keep taking my usual good and healthy diet.

Dr Mulholland further said that they will monitor the platelet counts every week till they reach the minimum eligible mark of 140K (per microlitre of blood). I was very sceptical that the platelets could bounce back that quickly.

When I discussed this with my sister over the phone, her comments were the similar - "if you keep taking the right nutrition and strictly iron-rich vegan diet for next 'few' weeks, you will definitely witness a big jump in the count- hence every night a spinach and tomato soup is must".

That's exactly what Anu did thereafter. Since I was very sensitive to tomatoes, Anu altered the recipe and fed me with organic spinach soup replacing tomatoes with lots of organic garlic and organic ginger, that I loved.

Clearly, in these circumstances, we did not have much of Christmas' 2016 and neither any New Year celebrations for 2017. I felt sad for my children; this was the second year in a row they had suffered because of me and had missed their Christmas celebrations.

A week later, I went for blood test again even though my instinct was that I should be going to blood tests every fortnight and not on the weekly basis because the count of 38 was indeed very low - albeit not to the extent where I would need 'platelet transfusion' which is typically given when the count reduces to red zone of under 15 mark.

On the date of next blood test, I knew the count would be low again, but upon meeting, Dr Mulholland informed me that the platelet count has actually started to increase, and they have come up from 38 to 52. Clearly, they were still not high enough for the chemo drug could be given.

On week 3, the blood tests results revealed similar trend my platelet count was 77, up from 52 this time. Later, I calculated that the rate of increase in past two weeks were 36.8% and 48% respectively. Clearly not only my platelet counts were increasing but also the 'rate' of increase was also going up. I decided to come up with projected platelet count for next week and took an estimate increase rate of

50%. With that rate, I estimated that my count should be over 115, very close the required minimum level of 140 and they should be easily in the required bracket a week after that. After accepting the fact that I still was going to wait for couple of weeks, I started to prepare myself mentally for chemo in two weeks' time and Anu as always continued to look after my nutrition.

When I went for the following week's blood test, the sample revealed completely astonishing result. Whereas I had anticipated a jump of further 50% and a count of 115 or close (but still short of the minimum requirement of 140), the actual jump was whooping over 87% that took the platelet count to 144. The Neutrophils too had increased into the safe bracket (2.0 against the required range of 1.8 – 7.7). I went hysteric in my mind and felt enormously great at that moment, though it was just a small win in bigger scheme of things. All my negative thoughts disappeared, and I started to feel triumphant yet again with such a simple result.

But my exuberance was very short lived. Just when I began to get excited Dr Mulholland proclaimed: "but …". I gaped at him.

"Your liver function test reveals toxicity in the liver and the hospital would have to refuse treatment again till the liver has recovered and the toxicity disappears".

That was a devastating news for me and shattered all my enthusiasm.

I had heard this earlier that if we take supplements without any specific reason, then instead of nurturing and strengthening the human body, they can actually have the opposite effect and can end up in building toxins in the body. Finally, the results were in front of me.

I had no option but to stop taking the supplements straightway. But I was feeling frustrated because clearly due to the delay in completing the Cycle 5, there was a knock-on effect on the starting of last cycle of the treatment i.e., Cycle 6.

I had reduced my diet to vegan, mainly green vegetables and spinach soups. No fruit would suit me at all – no apples or bananas, no avocado or grapes and certainly no berries of any kind. In fact, I had developed a big revulsion towards the dry fruits such as almonds, walnuts and cashew nuts, that I loved to munch in my pre-illness days. Overall, I can say that I had been surviving only on spinach soup and 'wholemeal Indian chapatti', with lots of organic garlic and organic ginger. I had a grave concern, what if my weight drops further and goes lower that 65kg as that would be a huge drop from weight of 83kg I had just before the diagnosis in 2015. I was turning into a skeleton and no garment would fit me. But hope kept me in the 'race' that I am almost at a finish line and once the Cycle 6 is over, I will get a rest period for three months and that will give me an opportunity to regain my weight and strength.

Finally, on March 16th, 2017, I went for blood test again and the sample showed a complete elimination of toxicity from the body and platelet and neutrophils held their respective counts to the previous levels. This time I had no strength to get excited, I just felt an immense relief.

I was given the dosage of final cycle of the PVC cocktail. But that was only in theory. In actual. I was only given a single agent Lomustine, the primary drug of the cocktail. I had no issue taking 120mgs of capsules and had a relief that I am free from the torture of chemotherapy, at least for some time. Dr Mulholland proposed an MRI scan in six weeks' time.

When Dr Mulholland had set the first scan on April 27th, 2017, I had started to unrealistically wish for the scan to come clear but at the same time I had started to prepare myself should my destiny decide to hammer me further; and the tumour fails to show any sign of regression.

Complementary Therapies

Not too far from my home is the centre of St. Luke's hospice. Maggie advised me that at the charity, I could get a range of complementary therapies that should assuage my pain I had endured during the chemo and with the therapies, I should feel better.

I had read a lot about the complementary therapies such as massage, acupuncture and other kinds of soft healing such as physiotherapy, which I already had when I was recovering from the surgery in India.

I began to look forward to visiting the centre. Just a couple of days later, I enrolled myself for all possible complementary therapies they could offer to me, given the state of my health.

I started with the 'relaxing' music therapy that was being performed by a very skilled and gentle musician named Allan Watts, who would perform music to other cancer patients and their carers every Tuesdays. Since I had always loved gentle music and had listened to Indian classical music, I began to look forward to enjoying his music. When I met Allan, he already knew about my condition, yet he still discussed my illness with me, and I conveyed what 'relaxation' music I like to hear. Allan understood everything and assured me that I am in right place. He later turned out to be very proficient in gentle performing of several instruments such a Tibetan Singing Bowl, Harp, Native American Flute, Monochord and last but not least an eight-string guitar. He would play such gentle and relaxing music that many people including myself would often drift to 'blissful' sleeps. Later, I bought the CD of the album he had recorded that I would put on my music system at nights.

Later, I met with the acupuncturist of the centre, Ruth Bony. She initially inquired about my interest and belief in acupuncture. She agreed to start the treatment and within few sessions it started to show positive results by relaxing my body.

Thirdly, to avail all possible services of the Hospice, I enrolled myself for sessions on physiotherapy and my therapist was very talented, Sarah Young. She gave me some gentle exercises to do that restored my physique to large extent and enabled me to join the gym later on.

I had started enjoying the impact of the therapies that I was receiving at St Luke's. Sound Therapy and Acupuncture would relax me immensely and physiotherapy had started to restore my physical strength. I always felt thankful to Allan, Ruth and Sarah for the healing and therapies that they had provided to myself and undoubtedly other people. If they had not relaxed my body, I would have failed to re-join the gym.

Scans

My mother had been concerned of my critical condition during the days of my platelet counts. She had been seeing me in pictures, I had been sending over emails and she wasn't convinced at all that I have been making any healthy recovery. She was determined to do her bit and had flew to us on in mid Jan 2017. A couple of weeks prior to that my mother-in-law had returned back.

Mother was quick on the job the following morning. She claimed that she needs to take a good care of me while she was here for next five months or so. In the morning, she unilaterally declared that we needed a plan to restore my physique and psyche. She had brought all the necessary tools with her to give me massage and physiotherapy. I was astonished to see her come fully prepared. She is my mother, but she is also a qualified beautician and runs her own beauty parlour back in Chandigarh. As a result, she is an equally good masseur and a physiotherapist as well. Of course, I couldn't have asked for more, because if I took massage outside, it would have costed me at least £30 per hour. Now I was going to get absolutely free treatment mixed with the motherly healing touch and affection that couldn't be secured at all by paying money.

With the stuff she brought with herself, she started to give massage in my head with the natural 'Ayurveda' oils.

My restoration resumed and every day she would scrub of a lot of 'burnt' skin, I had got due to chemo drugs, from my body. My weight loss has been her biggest worry. The massage continued for a number of days and the 'burnt' skin was getting exfoliated en masse.

I had started to feel much better with the scrubs and massage and physiotherapy. I did not feel like going for any other therapy outside. Soon my muscles became supple too and I started to go to gym to do very light exercises. At home, I would practice deep breathing and other gentle stretches to keep my flexibility intact, because the chemotherapy had made my bones and muscles very stiff. I had stopped going to St Luke's for acupuncture and physiotherapy and just continued with the music therapy; in fact, even mother accompanied me to the music sessions a couple of times.

However, one problem remained unaddressed and that was an extreme itch that I had developed all over the skin, halfway during my chemotherapy; and it would constantly trouble me at nights, no matter how much my skin got scrubbed during the day and no matter how much moisturising lotion I apply before going to bed. The skin was clearly damaged due to the onslaught of the chemo drugs and as I was forewarned. To repair the damaged skin, mother suggested that I should be applying calamine lotion on whole body.

I went to the nearby Pharmacy and bought a couple of calamine lotion bottles – for just £6. When I started to apply the lotion on the body, I started to get immediate relief. There onwards, I had started to apply the lotion all over the body in the night just before dropping off to bed. I continued with this for a couple of months till my skin was all repaired.

The reclamation of skin brought me big psychological relief as well and I decided to improve my diet even further. While mother looked after my physique, Anu began to cook the food of my choice, which was primarily based on organic root ingredients with no processed foods whatsoever. Every mouthful I took was nutrition, that of course included the home-made fresh fruit juice.

I also used to get craving for traditional food such as scrambled fenugreek (methi) with garlic, ginger, green chillies and asafoetida (hing) etc; bitter gourd (karela) stuffed with organic root ingredients; moolie parathas (stuffed with healthy seeds of flax, pumpkin); and last but not least shallow fried the fox nuts (popped lotus seeds) (makhana) with fresh green salad.

I grew up with, craving of this type of food and taste in my mouth. Even though I was served my favourite dishes, I knew I had to be cautious while eating and would eats in bits only, slowly and very carefully.

I stayed pure Vegan though and away from all the non-veg and dairy products because even the smell of them would trigger extreme nausea in me.

As the days and weeks passed by, I started to pick the weight to my relief and continued with gym for light exercise and started to get my muscular strength back. When my friend called me from Singapore, his comment was – "weight increase during cancer treatment sounds good news and it implies that the body is rightly taking nutrition from outside and is no more relying on the internal reserves". That comment raised my confidence even further.

Partial Remission

Finally, April 27th arrived. Even though I was feeling better and no symptoms or side effects of any drugs were bothering me, still I was part panicked and part curious to know my scan results. I wanted to know how much and in which direction I had travelled in the last 18 months; and so were my mother and Anu. On the scan day, mother wanted to accompany me to the hospital. Anu had arranged with one of her friends to pick Zoravar and Nimrat from school.

As always, the first step was to give my blood sample for blood test and then we had a scan appointment just after the lunch time at 1:30PM. We reached 15 minutes in advance for the scan time.

The scan ran for around 40 minutes stopping halfway to give an intravenous of the 'contrasting agent', that gave me an immense chill. But I knew I had to endure it and I stayed still. While I was undergoing the scan, mother felt nervous and had started to read verses from Sukhmani Sahib - the breviary of Sikhism holy scripture Guru Granth Sahib.

The scan must have lasted for 40 minutes. After changing into my normal clothes from the scan robe, I went to see Anu and mother at the waiting lounge. They informed me that Dr Mulholland and Maggie were also sitting with the scan team and had left just before I came out.

After the scan ended my appointment with Dr Mulholland was due an hour later. I was hungry and wanted to grab some lunch and after that Anu performed the hospital ritual and informed the reception that the scan was over and we would be waiting in the adjacent lounge, with cafeteria, till the appointment time. An hour later, my name was called by another nurse Julie and she showed me the way to the appointment room. I proceeded towards the room nervously and soon saw Dr Mulholland and Maggie also coming the same way. I saw them smiling and felt positive and all the nervousness disappeared. I just followed Dr Mulholland and Maggie into the room. The look on their faces was a strong signal to me that I was going to hear some good news. Dr Mulholland then broke the suspense and announced – "There is some good news for you".

Dr Mulholland continued – "Your treatment has responded, and the tumour is in partial remission now." He also added that I do not need to take any further treatment at least at this stage. Hearing that I won't have to any more chemo drugs gave me immense relief. Just then mother and Anu entered the room and they did not have to guess to much what the news could be – our faces were revealing it all. The ladies were confused who to hug first, me, the fighter patient or Dr Mulholland, who gave me a new span of life?

After all the lows and bumps of past two years, it was finally a great news!! A truly joyous moment even though it was not a complete removal of the tumour. I saw tears in mothers' eyes, and we all hugged each other.

That was the shortest meeting I ever had with Dr Mulholland and Maggie. We were too eager to go home. But Dr Mulholland advised that before we leave, I need to book another scan at the reception for 3 months later. He gave an appointment note along with a blood test form for July 27th, 2017. I immediately went to the reception, while mother and Anu were discussing my condition further with Dr Mulholland.

On our way back to home, I was joyous that I had survived and was officially in the population that is above the median survival of 15 months. I couldn't believe my luck. Anu was driving but in excitement wouldn't stop chattering. Mother was sitting in the rear seat and thanking 'God' non-stop throughout the journey for me.

We arrived home some 35 minutes later and first we broke the news to Zoravar and Nimrat. The kids were excited and immediately broke into a 'victory dance'. I called everyone in India to break the news. The families were over the moon as well. My father-in-law told me over the phone that he would open the finest bottle of 'Scotch Whiskey' as a toast to my health.

That night, in hyper-excitement, I found impossible to go to sleep. I could not believe that I am on the verge of getting a 'new lease' of life and my strategy of scurrying deeper into the survival curve had started to show results. My thoughts were wandering to what 'exactly' did Dr Mulholland said during the day and then there was also speculation of the further developments that lay ahead.

I decided to change myself as a person and vowed to try to correct all my weaknesses and wash all my sins in this new extended life. During this restlessness, I did not realize when exactly I went to sleep and all I remember that nobody bothered to wake me up. I woke up at 10:00AM in the following morning.

Within couple of days, the news finally sank into all of us and we were on the move again. Since I was feeling lot better and positive, I felt new vigour in Gym as well, but decided that I shall still continue to do very light exercise. Dr Mulholland had earlier recommended Yoga to me. The Gym fee that I was paying included free Yoga class every Monday and Thursday.

I took Dr Mulholland's advice and started to go to the Yoga class, but I did not fit well into the class. I forced myself to go into the session for four consecutive weeks and then finally concluded Yoga is certainly not my cup of tea and I just dropped off. I found much better in the Gym doing very light weights and light cardiovascular exercises. The exercises that I was doing were a kind of 'embarrassing' performance compare to what I used to do in peak of my performance. But I did not care for anything and just focused on my own 'regime' in the Gym.

Mother continued with the daily massage at home, albeit I had started to take a break for a day or two during the week because I had finally moved out of the red zone in my treatment. I did not want to trouble my mother too much either and realised after all she was also a human. I would only wait for her to call me or remind me for massage, yet she would call me five to six times in a week.

Mother's visa was due to expire soon and she had pre-booked her return ticket for 16th June. She wanted to make sure that she leaves me in best possible condition both physically and psychologically. She was keen to see my weight going above 80 kilos and was not happy with 79 kilos, I had at that point. A night before her departure, she made a stock of 'Punjiri[13]' for me, and instructed me to consume after her departure, which I was going to do.

---

[13]A famous sweet dish of Punjab – a cooked mixture of flour, some ghee, dark brown sugar, lots of dry fruits several healthy seeds of sunflower and pumpkin etc.

After getting assured from the April Scan, even though we were financially holding up, Anu took up a job , as she wanted to start moving forward again as a family.

Status Quo

Mother departed and a week later mother-in-law (MIL) arrived on June 24th, 2017 for the second time, with an aim to look after all of us and support Anu by taking over the homely responsibilities and chores, looking after the kids and of course to look after me as well as I was in no position as yet to be of much use around the house.

Mother-in-law is also like my mother and resumed her responsibilities Since this time, I had no chemo drug to take, I began to enjoy her cooking. My mother-in-law took extreme care of my diet and would feed me all the super foods five times a day.

I and Anu had taken the last scan in April as a reward for our tenacity in dealing with the crisis and we were genuinely feeling positive and optimistic for the future, even though the result had only shown the 'partial remission' and not 'complete elimination'.

But we wanted to celebrate the occasion in our own unique way. We wanted to expel the sad memories and traces of illness from the house and we began to make some renovations to the house by building a conservatory, a new garden and renovating my room altogether. I wanted to enjoy my family life yet again with Anu and my children

.

After few days, Anu's sister Mona also arrived from California with her children to spend some days with us. Her children are more or less the same age group of Zoravar and Nimrat and had their summer holidays. They did not mind the house, which was a construction site in the backyard, where conservatory was being installed and enjoyed their trip just by staying inside the house around me and finally left just 3 days before my next scan was due.

Though the scan was supposed to be on Thursday 27th July 2017, but for reasons unknown it was delayed by a week for 3rd August 2017. My first reaction was of disappointment but since all appointments, including with Dr Mulholland, had been shifted to 3rd August, eventually I settled down and accepted the reality.

The same process followed on Aug 3rd. Anu drove me for blood sample around 11AM. While I went for blood tests, Anu went straight to the scan centre to confirm that the scan is indeed booked for the day and is due at 1:30 in the afternoon. Only after the confirmation was made, I went ahead and gave my blood sample. Finally, I was called into the scan at 1:30 in the afternoon and the usual process began that lasted for 40 minutes scan, with intravenous of contrasting agent halfway and with usual chill in my whole body.

Moments later it was an appointment time with Dr Mulholland and Maggie. During the appointment, Dr Mulholland confirmed that the tumour shows no changes. It was again good news for me. Dr Mulholland further advised that I must continue to be good and carry on doing what I have been doing, i.e., eating a healthy diet combined with light exercise such as walk in the park etc.

He further told me that I will continue to have scans after each quarter and then after 6 months for a couple of years. He also informed that regular scans are going to be part of my life now onwards. This was because high grade brain tumours such as GBM have nasty tendency of making a comeback, making it essential to keep monitoring them. I absolutely had no problem with that.

I was so excited that I even forgot to book the 3-monthly appointment for the next scan, just collected the blood test result of the day from Maggie and came straight home. We had just entered and broke to news to everyone. Everyone was joyous, even though this time it was all anticipated.

Trip to India – October 2017

With two consecutive positive scans I underwent a stage of humility and had gone spiritual in many ways and had started to listen to spiritual and peaceful hymns written by our 10 'gurus' of Sikhism. Later, that turned into a desire to pay homage at the Golden Temple in Amritsar, Punjab, the spiritual seat of the Sikhs. I arranged to visit the Golden Temple and other nearby religious places.

Moreover, I also had incentive to catch up with my dearest friends, some of whom I had not met for many years.

Dr Mulholland had no problem to give me a 'fit to fly' certificate and we flew to Chandigarh on the night of 14th October and reached Chandigarh in the early morning of 15th October. With the money I had earned by working hard in London, I had bought a flat in the city and we wanted to stay there. Since Diwali was also falling on 19th October that year, we wanted to celebrate the festival in our own home/flat. The kids were joyous and so were their grandparents meeting them. I kept catching up with my friends in my flat and they kept coming to meet me.

A couple of days after Diwali, we made a trip to the Golden Temple in Amritsar and I decided to show India's train ride to the children and booked A/C chair cars, though one can easily challenge that real India cannot be seen from the expensive A/C coaches.

I was looking forward to visiting the Temple that I had only visited during my early childhood and I hardly had any recollection of that.

When we went to see the main temple the following morning, the gathering was over whelming at first look. But we kept our patience and kept dragging ourselves in the crowd as a snail pace. That was a new experience for the children, but they did not complain even a bit. Being their first trip to the temple they were just stuck with the awe of the temple's architecture and we all enjoyed the serenity of the place, in spite of being crowded, sitting on the steps of the reservoir that surrounds the actual 'golden' temple.

When we paid a brief visit to the temple, all my thoughts were connecting me with divinity and my mind was only chanting "Nirbhau, Nirvair" (No fear, no malice), the 'mool mantra' or an essence of Sikhism. Since I am not a practicing Sikh, this short slogan is the central philosophy of my life and an ultimate truth for my reasoning.

During the walk in the compound of the temple I spotted wall and building, that got severely damaged in year 1984 when the Prime Minister of India at that time, Mrs Indra Gandhi had ordered the much infamous attack, called

'Operation Blue Star' in early to mid-June 1984[14], on the temple to expel her fierce enemy Sant Jarnail Singh Bhindrawala (a leading militant Sikh leader) from the temple complex.

It was a long political tussle between the two giant figures of the time, that still have many, often conflicting, opinions across India – but had resulted into the unfortunate and immature assassinations of both of them.

When I saw the remnants of the tank and bullet shells in the walls and buildings of the compound – my only reaction was that I felt sorry for the tragic loss of human lives, loss of prestige of the Sikh religion (that has nothing to do with any sort of radicalism at all as it stands only for peace and harmony for all the people on the Earth) during those few gory days and years of the militancy in Punjab that followed after the unfortunate operation and lasted around a decade. I wished all that had not happened but did not mention a word to my children!

---

[14] We were based in Udaipur, Rajasthan at that time as my father was posted there. The even shook the country and Mrs. Indra Gandhi was to be assassinated by her Sikh bodyguards on Oct 31st, 1984 followed by big riots in Delhi and over a decade long terrorist movement in Punjab. However, during this period, Udaipur was to remain absolutely peaceful.

Towards the same evening, we caught the train back to Chandigarh and reached our flat in the mid-night and I felt immense relief that that I have paid my dues to the divinity that I always felt I owed, during my sickness.

On our journey back, I discussed the essence of our trip with Zoravar. He told held some curiosity in his mind about the religion of Sikhism. Being a smart kid, he inquired the obvious - "Dad who is our God?". I had to articulate the answer to this intriguing question and replied "Son, the founder of our Faith, Guru Nanak preached something called "Ek Onkar" - which literally means "One Infinite" - that further implies "The Universe or Cosmic is one and Infinite at the same time". His reply was - "Ah! I knew that Universe is infinite". Then out of my own curiosity, I introduced him about the basic tenet of the faith "Nirbhau, Nirvair" (No fear, no malice). He gladly accepted this a best "motto" to live life. Being an astronomy enthusiast, I knew in his mind he made connections with 'astronomy' and 'space', the subjects he loved.

He always held this burning desire in him to discuss astronomy and space with someone on the trip but did not find anyone to match his prowess.

Then a day later, my best friend from the MBA days, Harmeet Singh, made an offer to fly over and meet me from Ahmedabad, some 750 miles south of Chandigarh. When he arrived, after inquiring about my health and couple of drinks and dinner with some good laughs, he started to talk to Zoravar. He got instantly fixated with Zoravar's passion and knowledge of astronomy and both of them enthusiastically talked of several astronomical topics such as Stephen Hawking, Black Holes, White Holes, Singularity, Supernova, Parallel Universe, God and the God particle, Quarks, The Hadron Collider, String Theory and others. I wonder where did this little boy of mine get the energy to talk on the same subject so enthusiastically for 4 hours non-stop till 1AM in the night / early morning of the following day. I had always admired the talents of Harmeet, that had made him a successful entrepreneur, but that night I felt immensely proud of my own brood as well. It made me realise how my son has grown up last couple of years, while I have been suffering.

I took his intellect as a blessing from divinity, efforts of Anu and accepted it with humility. Harmeet departed in the early hours to catch the first flight back to Ahmedabad.

Finally, I had managed to talk about my experiences and share laughs with our families and my dear friends. However, Zoravar's and Nimrat's half terms were coming to an end, we were to come back home in London.

We concluded our trip with satisfaction and bid a farewell to our families and came back to our home on 29th October.

My next scan was due in just 3 days.

Stable Disease

This was the Scan I was really looking forward to. Right at the onset when I was proposed the scans by Dr Mulholland, within my mind, I had kept a condition of getting 3 consecutive clear scans, after which I would rate myself as 'fit' and 'normal' enough to move towards the long-term survival.

On 2nd November, I got ready early for the scan. There was no panic and no anxiety of any kind just a little curiosity to hear the verdict, wishing for the positive one, once again, so that I could declare myself 'officially' clear of the disease, at least for now.

We followed our usual routine. I went straight for blood test and Anu met me there after confirming the scan timing from the scan centre. After the blood test, I went for the MRI and the normal procedure followed for 40 minutes or so that included injection of contrasting agent, intravenously, halfway through the scan.

Later, I and Anu met with Dr Mulholland in his clinic. He congratulated me of another good scan and confirmed that now I have '*stable disease*'. I felt immense relief that my 3rd scan had also turned out to be all stable.

Dr Mulholland had started another clinical trial but suggested that since everything was stable now, he ruled out any benefit for me undergoing those trials. But I understood that should the 'tumour' show any signs of revival, then we had some options lined up. I congratulated Dr Mulholland and wished him best for the trials. When my GP, received the letter from Dr Mulholland, it had mentioned:

"Satinder is well. His MRI brain shows stable disease".
"I will see Satinder again in clinic in four months with a further re-staging MRI brain"

That was all assuring to me.

I had started to enjoy my life at last and had started to take interests again in my hobbies such as reading. I loved spending time with Zoravar and Nimrat. I was in love with Anu again after all the doom and gloom of over 25 months. Moreover, I was excited that I had finally qualified as a 'long term survivor' of GBM and I felt assured that my strategy to strive beyond the median survival of 14 months was working well-so far.

I was looking forward to keep crawling gently under the right end of the survival curve and prolong my life as much as I could. Ideally, I had set an aim of living a normal life span as if GBM had never entered in my head ever!

I called the families with exactly the same message and my resolution for the future. Everyone was pleased to hear my determination to survive and wished me well.

With those positive thought and wishes, I had resumed gym as well and had started to make myself stronger yet again.

Stable Disease continued

The next scan was due on March 1st, 2018. I did not think too much about it and just engaged myself in writing the first edition of this book and pursue gym to get my strength back.

The scan itself turned out as a mere formality and I went through the same process, yet again. In the scan letter from MVCC to my GP, Dr Gould, the oncologist representing Dr Mulholland had stated the following:

"The review of the imaging with the consultant radiologist has shown essentially stable disease. He[Satinder] will continue on surveillance and will be reviewed in four months' time with a repeat MRI and blood test"

Clearly, nothing unusual or unexpected in the report and it was just as expected. I decided to move my mind away from my illness for now and focus on other activities. But I did request a CD of the medical imaging from the Scan Centre, which I loaded on my computer along with the special medical imaging software to view the scans. I decided to include the scan image of the tumour in this book, as of the diagnosis in Oct' 2015 in Chandigarh and also the scan image of this latest scan. These images are captured in the next two pages.

I started to make good progress in gym but was still way short of the strength I had before I fell ill. Not ideal, but I decided to keep patience and just being regular to the gym. Very often, I would enjoy cooking as well, doing the school runs, taking care of Zoravar and Nimrat after their school and listening to Zoravar's commentary on space and Nimrat's chirping on various subjects, including 'grandmotherly' advices to me on how to look after myself during my illness.

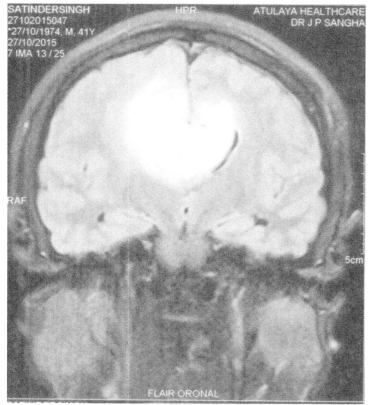

Scan Image 1 - Scan Image of Tumour, where the 'lump' of tumour is obvious. Scan Dated October 27th, 2015 at Atulaya Diagnostic Centre, Chandigarh, India.

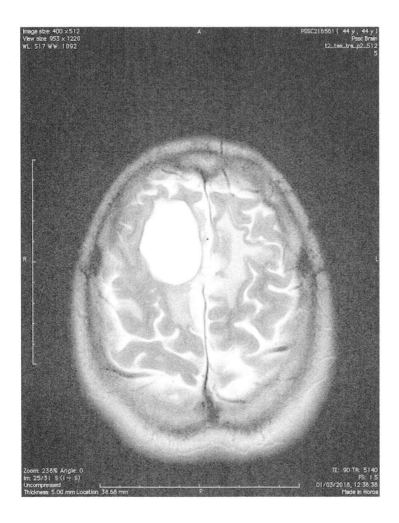

Scan Image 2 - Scan Image of Tumour 'Site', that is a cavity and could contain a mix of dead tissues of fluids etc. There is no obvious sign of tumour here. Scan Dated March 1st, 2018 at Paul Strickland Scanner Centre of Mount Vernon Cancer Hospital (MVCC), Northwood, London, UK.

Year 4 of Survival
New Chapter

Once I started to feel good about myself, I began to type the first edition of my book. I gave it a title "Life with GBM Brain Cancer: My Story and other essays" and self-published on Amazon. Since I had no marketing budget, I ended up publishing the book in limited locations only – wherever I had friends and relatives. And these countries were UK, USA, India, Canada, UAE, Singapore, Australia and New Zealand. The book was made available only in English language and further, the print editions were made available only in the UK and the USA. Everywhere else, I decided to publish the digital versions only (i.e., on Amazon Kindle).

Even though there was a very limited release of the book, I got an impressive sale (and feedbacks) of the book – mostly by the friends of my graduation and post-graduation days and close relatives too.

In the book, I had mentioned that after publishing it, I will move on to a Software venture and I did. I took my favourite idea from archived synopsis of 3-4 ideas, that I had compiled earlier during my working days. I finalised one and began to write code for a social networking website, which I had put live in middle of year 2019. Just like the book, I had no budget to propagate the site. I am relying only on my friends to kick start the site www.gdfnow.org but unfortunately, I could not push it well and struggled to get people to register on it en masse. However, it was a great learning experience for me because launching a website of that scale single handily had boosted up my moral. My programming prowess was back. Moreover, I felt that I could code and launch more websites.

The year from mid-2018 to mid-2019 turned out to be a bliss and the great year, ever since I had started to show the stress-depression like symptoms back in late 2012. During this year, I felt truly in good shape even though 3 monthly MRI scans were still going to be conducted on my brain (more on them, later in the chapter). I had a great time with my children Zoravar and Nimrat and spent lots of time with them. I missed them immensely during my illness and treatment days that lasted 4 years. Even though they we not far from me - but the illness did not permit me to go closer to them physically – to adore them or to hug them. I noticed they have grown in last 4 years, not only in physiques but also in their thinking, with more noticeable changes in Nimrat. I am glad, that they have developed positive values and wise thinking, while my attention was not on them at all! I give all the credit to my wife Anu and my love deepened even more for her.

In the meantime, Anu had made herself busy at work and I missed her at home, while children were at school. She is always incredibly busy in earning for the household, chores at home, looking after my health and last but not least, keeping the kids sharp in their intellect and spirit.

Zoravar continued to be keen in Astronomy and Space and had been making steady progress in the understanding of this field.

Nimrat on the other hand is a 'generalist' (all-rounder) in academics and is a wise young lady – very caring, yet sharp in her mind and body. She is amongst top two in the class and great at her school's gymnastics club. I always feel very proud of my brood.

The Scans continued

During this period, I had to undergo the MRI scans of my brain, after approximately after every 3-4 months. Since my scan dated 1st March 2018 had concluded a 'stable' disease, the subsequent scans were only meant for surveillance, because neither I nor my Oncologist wanted to take any risk.

Scan – June 20th, 2018

The scan was conducted in the usual manner and it turned out to be all fine, and as expected. Dr Mulholland's letter stated to my GP -

"Satinder is well, his MRI scan shows stable disease, in fact with some further minor improvements."

Seeing the good result Dr Mulholland decided to have a next scan in six-month time instead of 3-4 months. I felt a big relief with the words "further minor improvements". I felt deeply thankful to divinity and the medical sciences that seemed to be working in unison; and hag granted me a new lease of life. I decided that I must continue to be good and make the best use of "extended life" that I have got blessed with.

I had started to put lots of time on my project and would look for every opportunity to do the coding. It was taking a good shape and I was eagerly looking forward to completing the code and put it live soon.

During these months, I made also attempts to find free-lancing jobs in the city, to earn some extra cash for the family – to sponsor some holidays for all of us and fund extra-curricular activities for the children. However, I discovered, that even though I have been feeling great, but I was certainly not fully recovered as yet. I still had some impacts on my speech and my body, that had slowed down considerably; will continue to deter me from working the city for long hours and travelling underground at peak hours.

Then I decided to change my Resume and LinkedIn profile stating that I am available for work on software coding, but 'primarily have to work from home because of my limited mobility'. My profile continued to state that for these six months, but unfortunately, I did not get any call for 'work from home' positions. All interview calls I received were for the full-time employment, that I had to reluctantly refuse, only to feel guilty that I could not work as I really would have liked to. But then giving a positive spin to that, I continue to search for hidden blessing in disguise!

At back of my mind, I did have desire to get a part-time and work-from-home job, but apart from earning some extra cash to support Anu, there was no other real justification to hunt for a job – for primarily two reasons. First, I was hooked into my projects that I wanted to see them going live, and secondly, as I mentioned earlier, the incapacity to travel to the city at peak hours deter me from making wholehearted attempts. I decided to keep my nerves and continued with the development of my own internet projects and keep going for scans as and when they were due.

Scan – December 20th, 2018

After exactly six months gap, the scan was held on 20th December 2018. In his letter, Dr Mulholland reported -

"MRI scan shows stable disease. There was [in the scan] a tiny area of enhancement which is not likely to be significant, but we will arrange, and earlier restaging scan and we will see him again in three-month time".

This scan turned out to be bit different from the previous one, six months ago. Even though Dr Mulholland had stated "not likely to be significant" but in the same note, he had further mentioned - "but we will arrange an earlier restaging scan again in three-month time". I had understood that all this 'enhancement' is due to the hyperactivity of my brain taking stress to find job.

The obvious message from Dr Mulholland got restated to me - "I will continue to be under observation". With that message, my enthusiasm that had soared back in June scan had dimmed a bit. I collected myself and concluded firmly that my illness is something that would never disappear but is something that I have consistently manage to stay well.

At last, I had found blessing in disguise as well. I realised, if I did not get the job, then the destiny clearly has something else planned for me. I started to look for alternate opportunities they are knocking my 'back door'. I discovered all the ideas that I was meant to implement are those opportunities in reality.

Eventually, I decided to finally burn the bridges and decided to move on my own way. I decided to continue working on my own ventures and decided that I shall not trouble myself into the same kind of working environment where I had spent 15 years of my career. I discussed this with Anu, and she was fine with me to 'move forward' and not to 'look back'. I concluded the world has infinite possibilities and I need to care form my health for now, and if I continue to keep advancing on my ventures, they will surely land me somewhere, sooner or later. Anu stated that she doesn't mind continuing to earn bread for the family in the meantime and as always promised her support to me in whatever venture I choose.

With that reasoning, I began to look forward to the forthcoming scan in March 2019. In the meantime, I and Anu gave notice to our gym and bought an integrated home gym, that I and Anu started to use almost every day. The home gym turned out to be better for me. Not only it costed us less on monthly basis, but there was much flexibility of time and efficiency in doing the exercises as well. My trip to the gym otherwise has been costing me over 2 hours and now at home I could finish my exercise in just 45 minutes – with flexible timing as well.

India Trip – Feb 2019

It was time to make another trip to India and we landed in Chandigarh on 10th February 2019. The highlight of the visit this time was the stay of 5 nights in Rajasthan mostly in Udaipur, also called as "City of lakes", because half a dozen or so lakes are the highlight of the city.

I had proposed the trip to Anu's family, because the city is very special me. I had done most of my primary schooling in the Central School (Kendriya Vidyalaya), that was based right inside the Army area. My father-in-law booked a trip for all of us and we reached the Army guest house on 14th February, the day when Indian security personnel were attacked by the terrorists in Pulwama, a territory in the troubled state of Kashmir. My father-in-law got really concerned because India had lost 40 soldiers of the paramilitary forces. It was bit upsetting, but the government had vowed to take revenge from the terrorists, who usually infiltrate from neighbouring territory in Pakistan. That statement from India's Ministry of Defence gave some relief to my otherwise tense F-I-L and next morning, we began to explore the key attractions of the city, starting from my school where I had studied. We explored the key tourist attractions of the city and I took Anu and Zoravar for dinner to my favourite restaurant of the childhood days, where we enjoyed Rajasthani cuisine and, on our way, back to the guest house, we took a detour through the area where we used to live in those days.

We left Udaipur and enroute to Chandigarh, we stopped for a night in a small but highly significant town for Indian history named Chittorgarh. After seeing the main fort, we continued with our journey and arrived back in Chandigarh on the night of February 19th and spent rest of the days with my parents. After catching up with my siblings, cousins and friends, for a week or so, we flew back to London on February 28th, after enjoying yet another memorable holiday in India.

After settling down, I just eagerly looking forward for my next MRI that was due in 3 weeks' time.

Scan – March 21st, 2019

The scan surprised me again, but this time for good. The *'tiny area of enhancement'* that was reported in the earlier scan seemed to have backtracked. Dr Mulholland had reported -

"The MRI scan shows stable disease, and we will see him again in the clinic in four months with a further restaging MRI brain".

That was good news for me. I started to explore the possible activities that I can undertake, now that I was free from any illness. I was watching Anu working incredibly hard for the family. I felt like giving some financial support to her by joining some job again, in spite of my earlier claims that I had 'burned the bridges'.

My first website, that I had developed single handily, was taking good shape and as mentioned earlier, I was looking forward to launching it, which I did, albeit there were very few members who had registered on the site.

Since, I was still a 'physically challenged' person, I did not want to become a liability on a potential employer. Instead, I started to seek a relatively 'junior developer' position in London, with an intention to take less load on myself and moreover, the title did not matter to me anymore. The only objective was only to support Anu and I knew that salary I get would not be a criterion for me. I was thinking of taking a junior position with further intention of going extra mile to deliver more to my employer and exceed their expectations. That way I was hoping I would be able to support Anu in pulling the household cart with relative ease and by working together we can re-attain the lifestyle we had when I was working alone amongst us in the financial markets.

I had applied to couple of recruitment agents, but in vain. I did not get any interview call. I realised this has to be a competitive market that my CV was not selected by any potential employer. Getting dis-hearted was not an option and I decided to meet my ex-boss at JP Morgan, Chris, who had established himself a leading VAT Consultant in the Financial Market. When I met with him over the drinks one evening, I concluded two things:

Firstly, Chris as always, assured me that he will look around for opportunities for me and would without hesitation recommend me to some good financial house and the top recruitment agents who specialize in the Financial Markets. But he advised me, that since my best experience had been in the VAT area, realistically, that's the area where I would get an employment. It was not ideal for me, since I wanted to go technical. However, having worked in the VAT of the Investment Bank, I knew I should be able to find something in that space. I agreed with Chris and I was ready to reconsider position in the VAT area. In fact, Chris had launched his own VAT Consulting firm brucegatevat.com and offered me a position of IT head in the firm, which I gladly accepted on spot.

Second, on the flip side, my travel to the city had been very challenging that evening. Since I had commuted in the rush hour in the evening, my instinct told me that I won't be able to cope up with the travel like this every day. While I was perfectly fine while working from home in my own room, travelling in London underground, turned out to be completely different story. By the time I reached home, I had made my decision. I concluded that it was a mistake on my behalf to even consider working in the city full time. When I look back, I realise that I had not fully comprehended the phrase 'burning of bridges'.

The next morning, I decided to look for a 'work from home' IT job and again I wasn't bothered with the salary I get. I changed my LinkedIn profile to reflect this new status. Unfortunately, however, I forgot to mention to Chris about the change of decision that I had made after our meeting. The following week, I received two calls from leading VAT recruiters from the city, looking to hire professional like me for the leading financial institutions. Since, I had already made up my mind, I conveyed to them "No doubt, I am willing on the positions (they were proposing), but after a few days of working on the site, I would like to work from home majority of the time: and only occasionally travelling to the office". I do not know how my decision was perceived by them, but they never contacted me again. At this point, I called Chris and updated with the decision. He agreed with me that health is paramount and if my body does not permit, I must not take hassle to travel to the city.

I updated my CV (and LinkedIn profile) and waited for calls to "work from home", which I never received.

Moreover, during this period I got another complication that put me in worry for a short period. I had started to get some blood suspended in my serum (called Haematospermia). On first occasion, I was confused but on the second occasion, I got concerned and booked an appointment with my GP. The GP checked my history and referred to the local Northwick Park Hospital, where I had gone after the collapse on the street back in September 2015.

At the hospital I went to Urology clinic, headed by Mr Webster. The clinic did my blood test, serum test and a digital rectal examination. They wanted to clarify that I have no 'prostate cancer'. They also performed thorough examination of my blood, urine and semen to establish or rule out any chances of 'prostate cancer'. Again, that gave me troubled time for a week or so till I received the final reports. However, I was asked to watch out the serum and advised me if it is just an infection, I should get clear serum soon, because that is generally the case with Haematospermia. Incidentally, to my relief, the blood suspension had stopped, and the tests had also established that it was just a case of 'minor infection'.

After this relief, I waited for my next scan and to distract myself towards something constructive, I sped up the testing of the portal, that I had put live (the 'alpha[15]'

---

[15] A very limited release of the software amongst the close friends to give it a proper test.

version) in the beginning of June 2019, under the domain name of www.gdfNow.org.

Scan – July 25th, 2019

The scan was performed on July 25th. Though I was feeling absolutely fine, with no symptoms at all, but the report I was going to have was holding a small element of surprise for me. After I had got three 'clear' consecutive scans, my hustle and bustle of various activities such as searching for job, looking after my kids, scare given by Haematospermia and on top of that my own project had unfortunately made to take my eyes off the healthy nutrition. Even though I was eating healthy diet, but in my condition, I was meant to eat 'super healthy' diet. Basically, everything that I have consuming during my illness, I should have continued with it. It all got obvious when I met Dr Mulholland. His letter mentioned –

"On reviewing the scans over the years [since the first clear scan], it can be seen that there is a very minor growth in the tumour, but we are going to continue surveillance".

Dr Mulholland had mentioned the same thing to me in person earlier. When I asked if I am going to undergo further treatment he refused and said -"All you have to do is to restore the daily regime that you had followed during the treatment – healthy eating and light exercise and calm mind, and we should see the better results next time".

That was a convincing argument no doubt - and I took it as a wakeup call. I finally reiterated once again to myself that my illness is certainly not the one that can be completely eliminated, but something that I have to manage on day-to-day basis for "rest of my life".

The same evening, I was in action and ordered all the super stuff from the 'super food' shops on the Internet. Anu went to superstore and brought in all the fresh essential fruits and vegetables - all organic.

In the meantime, I received an appointment from the Urology clinic in the Northwick Park Hospital. During the appointment, they gave me all clear – nothing to do with GBM and neither any sign of prostate cancer. It turned out to be an immense relief for me, but I did learn the lesson that I need to be 'extremely careful' as far as my health (physical and mental) is concerned.

I decided to finally burn the bridges and conclusively decided that I shall never go for any job but will only work on my own projects. In spite of my own indecisiveness, Anu as always was fully supportive of my decisions and I had started to explore further ideas from the archive and this time I was looking for something that I can passionately follow for rest of my life. In the meantime, I started to sharpen my software skills further because I knew whatever I do, it will be some kind of software implementation. Finally, I updated the LinkedIn status to "Self Employed", because I knew that update would deter the job agents from approaching me. I felt relieved that at last, I had stepped out of the hamster wheel and had freed myself to pursue my own dreams!

Zoravar continued to be keen in Astronomy and Space and had been making steady progress in the understanding of this field. In fact, he surprised me when we watched live telecast of ISRO's[16] Chandrayan 2 mission to the moon.

---

[16]Indian Space Research Organisation

When the landing failed, he gave his theory that Vikram, the lander, has not been accurate on the projected path while lowering on the lunar surface. In making attempts to auto correct the trajectory, it lost its fuel and at the time of making a smooth landing from an altitude of 1km or so, it ended up making a hard landing, that too off from the actual spot it was meant to land and got tilted as a result of that. I was surprised with his sense of observation and the proposed theory was impressive too, given that he was just 11 years of age.

Still, I was looking forward to my next scan, that was booked for October 21st, 2019. I just pressed on with my healthy diet, several proofs of concepts of new technologies for web development and enjoyed my time with my children.

Scan – October 24th, 2019

The scan again turned out to be 'all clear'. I attributed this success to the diet plan that I had tuned following the words from Dr Mulholland in the previous scan.

I had further suggested to myself, yet again, that there is no thing called 100% elimination of the illness, I am having; but a condition that I have live with for rest of my life and I have to constantly manage myself and stay on alert all the time to get consistent results. I knew it would be a great challenge to live that way, but the zest for life is lot more than the great challenge to keep Cancer at bay.

Also, a blessing in disguise – my own free time to push the software projects without any external pressure – and a big realization at last that I am master of my own destiny and captain of my own soul.

Scans 2020 – 2021

Year 2020 was not only a beginning of a new year for me, but it was a new decade as well and made me think and plan for the whole decade. I have covered the details in the chapter "Awakening" ahead but let me summarize the other key events that took place during this period.

I was waiting for the first scan of the decade/year that was due on January 23rd, 2020. During this wait, I received an email from my alma mater in Chandigarh (India), Punjab Engineering College. The college was planning to celebrate the silver jubilee of our batch, that passed out in 1995, on Saturday, February 15th, 2020. Since it was going to be great opportunity to meet many old friends and batchmates after 25 years, I had said yes to the invitation and booked my return tickets. My family was to stay back because of Anu's office and kids' schools, I had intentionally kept it a short trip of 2 weeks. Incidentally, that was the time when the news of global reach of Coronavirus had started to spread. Since these were the early days and it was not clearly a pandemic as yet, I decided to go ahead albeit with all the precautions that were being prescribed by the UK and the Indian governments and booked the ticket from Heathrow departing February 8th. But some of my friends in USA and Australia had called off their trips due to Corona scare. I had to call one of my friends in Australia to convince him – "If we take all the precautions, I don't see any risk of catching the virus". My friend was convinced, and he promised me to meet at the event.

In the meantime, I continued to be under the care of Dr Mulholland, and we had started to build mutual respect for each other. While I was impressed by his expertise, knowledge and the personal attention he paid to my treatment, his argument for liking me was "if all other patients can hold the positive attitude like you have, and follow a healthy lifestyle that you have, that can make my job so much easier".

Also, I had entered the 6th year of survival that was going to reflect on his profile as well, because making it to 6th year is considered as long-term survival and no statistics of the Brain cancer survival of patients get published beyond six years. Moreover, since the graph by UCLA (reproduced below) did not show any figures beyond the sixth year, my strategy of scurrying under the curve for maximum possible survival was working very well so far.

With that mutual trust in each other, I was going to undergo the scans from January 2020 onwards.

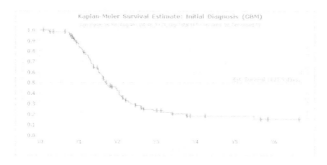

Fig 2: Estimated survival time of GBM patients. Source- UCLA

January 23rd, 2020

Dr Mulholland reported the following result of my January 23rd, 2020 scan to my GP:

"Satinder attended the neuro-oncology clinic today. He is feeling very well.

He has had an MRI scan which shows stable disease, and we will see him again in the clinic in 4 months' time with a new scan."

I had informed Dr Mulholland about my upcoming travel and he clearly had no objection to that.

I caught my flight on 9th and was in Chandigarh in the afternoon of February 10th after taking connecting flight from the Delhi airport. I was impressed with India's preparedness ahead of Corona as all the staff and workers on the Airports were wearing face masks and have been taking all the precautions, they could. My instinct was Corona would fail in India, but clearly, I was going to get shock of my life in quarter 2 of 2021, when India ran out of oxygen supplies due to overwhelming Corona cases.

My parents had come to the Chandigarh airport as I was going to stay with them during my trip. The next day my best friends came to pick me for drive in the city and we discussed the party that had been arranged by my exclassmates on the 14th night, a night before the main official event.

I had a wonderful time on the evening of the 14th, and it was great to meet many of my course mates after 25 years.

Even though the alcohol and dance floor were open, but my health would not permit to consume much liquor or to step in to move my body. I ended up staying on a table and met and greeted people on the seat only. Around 1:00 AM, I requested one of my friend to drop me at home, but the party was to go on till 4-5 AM in the morning.

In the excitement of meeting my old friends, I had completely forgotten that it was Valentine's day as well and I should have called Anu back home, but as always, she turned out to be very considerate and later conveyed to me that she wanted me to just enjoy my much earned time with my friends.

The next day was the main event where I met lots of other batch mates who were not present at the party the previous night. We were given a tour of the campus and I spotted several changes in the facilities that were available

162

to the students. The computers department had expanded considerable and my niece who was in the third year of her degree escorted me to show the modern facilities that had and all the latest software books and journals in the library. I was impressed, because during my days, there was not that much of a glamour in the computers department. Apart from Windows 93 that was launched during my days, that had established Bill Gates as the hero for all the students of modern IT / Computing technologies, there was nothing else I could recall.

But now, 25 years later I could feel the vibrancy of the success of India's software industry in the air. I could imagine, why my niece was feeling thrilled. She had a strong instinct that she has bright future ahead and I was happy for her.

After the meet, my In-Laws wanted to entertain me as well and since my Father-In-Law is a retired Brigadier of Indian army, he wanted to take to a nearby, Himalayan resort named Kasauli, and we spent night in the Army accommodation. I enjoyed an evening drink with him and as always enjoyed listening to his war stories.

I left Chandigarh on Feb 20th, as I had promised my best friend during the MBA, Harmeet to spend a night at his place in Delhi. He came to receive me at the airport, and we had a good laugh during the evening and at the dinner. The following morning on 21st Feb, Harmeet dropped me Delhi airport. That concluded my short but very memorable trip to India. Three weeks after my landing, in the mid-March 2020, UK announced the lock-down due to global COVID pandemic. I felt glad that I had made my trip in time.

When I reached home, it was time to resume the study of various subjects to broaden my knowledge and at the same time, I was waiting from next scan that was due in mid-May.

May 21st, 2020

The scan was performed as usual, but unfortunately, it did not go as smoothly as me previous scans. Under the machine, I had started to suffer nausea when the contrast agent was injected into my body. Though a buzzer is always at disposal to the patient, to be used in any emergency, but I decided to endure the nausea and decided against pressing it, neither did I tell any staff, as it had withered away just 10-15 minutes after the scan.

Dr Mulholland called me the following week on May 21st, 2020 and reported the following to my GP.

I had a telephone consultation with Satinder today. He is well. His MRI brain with contrast dates 14th May 2020 shows stable disease. We will see Satinder again in clinic in four months with a further restaging MRI brain with contrast.

September 15th, 2020

My next MRI was booked for 15 September 2020 at 10:30 AM. After a hearty breakfast at 9AM, I dressed up to leave. As usual, Anu drove me to the scan centre. By then I had completely forgotten about the nausea episode I had back in May. But this time, the contrasting agent troubled me very severely. Whereas, the reaction was moderate in the previous scan, it was lot more violent this time (and primarily because I had consumed the breakfast just 45 minutes before the scan). I had no strength to carry out the scan till the end and pressed the emergency button just few minutes after the contrasting agent had spread into my body. A minute later, I suffered from extreme bout of vomit and threw out all of my breakfast in a vomit bowl. I was feeling extremely sick and unable to move. The radiographers, for the precaution sake, did not give any medicine to me. Instead, they called the doctor on duty. The doctor checked me and declared the obvious that it was an extreme reaction that the contrasting agent gave to my body. He too prescribed no medication to me and advised the staff that since the stomach is all empty now, they can resume the scan after 30mins or so, and they did. I was also feeling OK under the scanner this time.

My clinic date with Dr Mulholland was on September 24, where I told everything about the most unpleasant experience, I had in the scan machine. Dr Mulholland reported the following:

Mr Singh attended the clinic today along with his wife. He is feeling well in himself and reported no new symptoms. He remains on the same dose of Keppra as he was the last time, we saw him. I informed him that his MRI scan from September has shown stable disease and no signs of any recurrence. He did admit that he had issues with the contrast the last time he had the scan. He was violently sick after the contrast was injected and tis had happened to him in the previous scan as well. I explained, this is likely and intolerance to the contrast. I have given him Chlorpheniramine and Metoclopramide that he can take prior to the scan. I have also noted this on MRI request so that the Scanner Team are aware of this.

We picked the prescription from the hospital pharmacy and I was going to taking the recommended dose of medicine, along with a precaution of nothing to eat or drink two hours before the scan time.

December 24th , 2020

The next MRI was performed on 24th December 2020. This time, I knew that I had to take the dose that was prescribed by Dr Mulholland and obviously I had not forgotten the torture I had endured under the scanner. The scan this time had to be normal as I had taken all the precautions that included not consuming anything for 3 hours prior to the scan. The good result was reported by Dr Mulholland to my GP in the following words:

I had the pleasure of speaking to Mr Singh over the telephone today. He continues to feel well in himself and has stayed on the same dose of Keppra 500mg bd since his operation in 2015. He has no symptoms whatsoever since the last time we spoke. I was pleased to inform him that the scan that he had done on 24th December was shown to be stable with no new lesions. He was pleased to hear this. I explained to him that we will speak again in three months' time.

May 6th , 2021

Dr . Mulholland had reported:

"I met with Satinder and his wife. We were joined by Dr Wu. Registrar in Medical Oncology. Satinder is feeling well. His MRI brain shows stable disease. We will see him again in the clinic in four months, with another MRI brain with contrast

We talked today about some of the challenges of living with the long-term consequences of having the treatment for brain cancer. I have given them the contact details of the Charity Brainstrust who are an organisation for patients and their carers"

The "challenges of living" that I discussed with Dr Mulholland were twofold:

First, I mentioned to Dr Mulholland that as much as I try to be active, I struggle to travel on London public transportation, primarily the London underground. The discussion concluded on the note that since I wasn't going to take job in the city, that should not bother me and as and when I need to meet my ex-colleagues turned friends, I can always travel during the mid-day (non rush hours) and meet them for lunch. This started to work well for me, and I started to travel to the city after every two weeks to catch up with my ex-colleagues. Of course, this all got interrupted big time due to Corona lockout in London.

Second, Anu with her best of intention had bought a cocker spaniel puppy for the family - thinking that while she was at work and kids at school, the puppy dog could be my companion. Kids were obviously very happy to have dog as their play companion, but as she grew; in couple of months, she started to bark as dogs would normally do. Unfortunately, however, her barking had started to raise my anxiety, which clearly was not a good sign for my health.

When I discussed this situation with Dr Mulholland, his advice was if I am getting troubled by a 'dog', then I should become like a 'cat'. Even the cats do not like the noise and whenever the loud sounds upset them, they just withdraw from the situation and whisk away to the calmer places to relax.

That instantly gave me a grand idea – I can become like a cat and I had a place as well where I could find peace - my garden house.

A couple of days later, I hired a skip to throw away all the unwanted clutter from the garden house and a week later, after refreshing it, I had move to my new "man's cave", along with my Mac and broadband connection.

Yet another discussion was the contact I had been given by Dr Mulholland. I checked their website and decided to introduce myself to them with an updated edition of my book and I started the second edition in my new 'accommodation'.

September 9th, 2021

Dr Mulholland had fixed the next scan date to September 3rd, 2021. I set an aim to be more productive in my new room and shall aim to publish this second edition of the book along with the Hindi version of my website www.bjmanch.in (more details in chapter "Awakenings" ahead).

Awakening in new Decade
New Chapter

The new year 2020 was also a start of new decade for me. I ended up strengthening my spirt and will power 10 times more to live with an aim of creating at least 10 innovations in the new decade to make this world a peaceful place to live in for the whole humanity along with its flora and the fauna. Since, my first clear scan, I had started to widen my knowledge of the world that we live in and acquainted myself in several subjects apart from autobiographies/biographies of great men and women.

I got hooked with Philosophy as a subject and my eagerness made me read the western philosophy and was very impressed with Socrates of ancient Greece and his two generations of pupils Plato and Aristotle. Aristotle had elated my spirits when I read about his concept of Eudaimonia in his classic book 'The Nicomachean Ethics'. The concept of eudaimonia had touched me very deeply when I realised that there is something more than happiness that could be an objective of our lives, because eudaimonia literally means - it is "an activity of soul in accordance with virtue". I did not have to look any further because I had all I had to do was to find something that is close to my heart and on which I can work for rest of my life, i.e., finding work of life and for life. I experienced a new awakening and a new level of meaning of our lives. But I also knew that I really have to scrutinize my ideas and decide which one can appeal me for next 100 years, if I was supposed to live that long.

At the same time, I got fascinated with Sir David Attenborough of the UK and his unwavering dedication to save and serve environment of our planet Earth. I did not read any of his books per se but would watch his TV documentaries for hours till I could feel his passion for nature. Whenever, I would sit in front of my TV, I would scroll through all the documentary channels and would find his documentary being broadcasted at least on one of the channels. His 2020 documentary film, *"David Attenborough: A Life on Our Planet"*, is also his personal witness statement of his life and the future. When I watched it, it was so impressive that it left me in awe!

He dedicated almost all of his adult life for the cause that was close to his heart and in the age of 95 he is pursuing his new mission with complete zest to support the environmental causes across the globe. If he is not a living legend than what else, he could be? I thought!

With these two grand inspirations in my spirit, I knew, I would also find my own eudaimonia very soon. I started to read books and articles voraciously to find an idea that I could pursue for rest of my life with passion!

But this new awakening had also brought with it a big dejection in my mind. Why did we humans stopped caring for our own mother planet Earth? Why do we hate and why nations go for war? What is terrorism and what for?

My research into the basis of humanity made me explore the ideologies that control/govern the humans. I became fully convinced with Democracy and the concept of free markets where every soul of this world is free to be creative enough to participate in the global trade and hence global welfare of humanity. Moreover, when I further read about Abraham Lincoln's conviction that "Democracy is government of the people by the people and for the people". It made me reflect further that democracy is not only important for human development but is also the noblest possible socio-political institution.

Without delving into details of a particular instance, I assume everyone is aware that with some rare exceptions, the Political parties and politicians all over the world jeopardise the institution of democracy, instead of strengthening it.

That made me question further – "Are political parties and politicians really essential for democracy"? I kept pondering but kept concluding that they may be needed in the bygone eras, but in the present age of Information Technology driven world where we are one the verge of en masse uses of Artificial Intelligence, and where all the possible information of not only our Planet but also of the Universe is at our finger tips, we definitely do not need Political Parties to deliver us their flavour of democracy, that have tendency to live in past and darg citizenry also to the past instead of directing them to the future; to divide humanity on the lines of race, color, religion, class and other dogmas instead of binding them globally for a shared and better future.

I further reflected, if IT and AI can take central place in democracy and if citizens of the world can adopt the social networking as their peaceful mean of coming together, sharing and learning ideas and plan the common future for the whole humanity, we can get rid of all real problems from the world. Of course, the key was empathy that every human needs to have and I am firm believer that we all are same under our skins and under the artificial layers of our identity such as race, religion, region or even nationality.

On the Internet one evening, I read that in ancient civilizations of India and Greece, there used to be system of direct democracy in small towns where the residents would come together and debate and discuss the key issues amongst them and agree on the resolution(s) that we meant to be binding on all the citizens. Only with time, as the populations grew in the regions and with the establishments of the cities, the direct participation of the citizens became impossible and instead the 'voodoo' ideologies such a left-wing or right-wing were created and soon political parties took birth and started to align with these political ideologies, that were to give rise to what we popularly call 'electoral democracy'.

They (the parties) with utmost zeal rushed to convince masses to buy their ideologies, broadly speaking so called Capitalism of the USA style on one extreme and Communism in/around Russia on the other extreme. Countries like India, that had a great mix of 'psyches' of population on the basis of religions, regions, languages, classes and castes, it was not possible to adhere to these ideologies in strict sense and the political system ended up in confusions and misfunctioning, benefitting no one but the politicians and their families and friends at the expanse of mass of humanity that was kept in intellectual darkness, regression and ignorance i.e., without any 'real' development of the masses. The informed and reasonable persons were certainly there but very few.

====

Once I was convinced of this thought, my mind prompted me to code my new venture of Internet based discussion forum, where users should be able to discuss, contribute and vote on key issues that the society face. I started to see the good old days of direct democracy revived for very large populations with an aid of Internet based technologies.

Since, I have been more conversant with the confusions of the political turf of my mother-land, my country of birth – India, I launched such as portal as a second venture (first being www.gdfnow.org) for India and named it 'Bhartiya Jantantra Manch' (Indian Democratic Front) and launched it as a site www.bjmanch.in in the autumn of year 2000. I had started to advertise it simultaneously on Facebook, where I started to see dozens of likes every day. I am well aware that the changing the future for 1.3-1.4 billion people is not going to an instant fix, so I made these projects to run for long term, and I knew I have to keep patience for as long as it takes for the concepts of these portals to sink into our masses. That made me publish first two blogs on the website: with Titles 'India – Future Growth Model' and 'Indian Economy- Post Corona'[17].

====

----

[17] https://www.bjmanch.in/info/Blog.xhtml

Yes, there have been abrupt upheavals in the middle east during the previous decade, popularly known as "The Arab Spring", where masses thought that they could overthrow the dictators and establish democracy overnight. Alas, all this started with a tiny success in Tunisia but ended with utter disaster in Syria. Moreover, I never believed in such passionate uprisings because generally these kinds of 'emotive' protests die down in relatively early stages, without bearing any fruits of success for the common people, as was obviously witnessed later on, especially in Syria.

I am firm believer of peaceful movements of the likes of Mahatma Gandhi and Martin Luther King Jr. and I was glad that I was conversant with software coding, via which I could launch the social networking website. That is the reason that I am patient for slow and gradual reforms to steer Indian Democracy towards prosperity for all its citizens.

Moreover, I knew that the concept of political and social freedom is not alien to the Indian populace, I wouldn't mind if the objective that I have set are not met within my lifetime. But it gives me a great satisfaction that I have set the ball rolling and in right direction too, to attain my eudaimonia!

I also take pride that I have initiated an innovative platform for democracy for the 21st century and beyond – The Internet!

====

One of India's own spiritual leader of late 19th century, Swami Vivekananda also inspired me, who was extremely kind hearted and passionate, but died at a tender age of 32. While Aristotle convinced me of eudaimonia as a mean to get to the ends, but I found that end in Swami Vivekananda's teaching. His most convincing argument was of *"Vedanta as the ultimate spiritual and social system that suits humanity's core nature"*. An ardent advocate to eliminate evils that prevailed in the world in general and in India in particular, such as superstition, illiteracy, caste system, untouchability, child marriage and many others, he proclaimed very convincingly that world's salvation lies in understanding the essence of Vedanta, that defines infinite

Cosmic (Brahman) and its infinite spirit or soul (called Ātman in Sanskrit). Vivekananda also convinced how the great saints and ascetics in India – from Gautam Buddha, Adi Shankaracharya and Guru Nanak propagated nothing but the essential message/philosophy of Vedanta in their own unique ways, hence binding the whole humanity of the subcontinent with a common 'spiritual' philosophy, the humanity that is otherwise deeply religious and has religion as the primary force behind the conduct of its affairs.

Next, I read biography of Albert Einstein by Walter Isaacson. Even though I did not grasp his theories of Special and General Relativities, but one theory that convinced me was - rather very large dimension of our "spherical" Universe, which is expanding and what lies outside of it would be a "crazy and useless speculation", because that is something that can never be explained! Einstein also proved that if the Universe does not expand, then it will not stay static, but will begin to shrink under the forces of gravity.

For some strange reasons, an idea flashed in my mind, that there is no 'physical entity' called God, that we traditionally/religiously we refer to. In the vast expanse of the Universe (and expanding too), lies the ancient Vedanta concept of infinite 'Brahman' (the eternity) and its infinite 'Ātman' (soul). I was glad our heritage wisdom was getting backed by the new inventions and discoveries of science.

That made me further convinced from Swami Vivekananda's proposition that Vedanta is the way forward and all the socio-political ideologies we know from Capitalism to Communism (and other confusions in between) are nothing but the illusions of human brain, where we 'think' that they are meant for the welfare of the masses, but in reality, they are the tools of "Power and Greed" for the few.

That started to make me restless to launch my vision as a website www.bjmanch.in but I knew, I have to stay patient. However, in order to expedite the reach of the site to the India masses, I had translated it into Hindi, India's national language and of our ancestors. I made it available at www.bjmanch.in/hi.

I aim to work on this website for rest of my life and strive to educate the masses on the merits on "Internet", effectively "Direct" Democracy. As the Internet savvy Indian population grows in future, I knew they would have a perfect tool for Democracy to enjoy their lives!

Part 2 Essays

Research and Learnings

In Part 2 of this book, I would like to share the notes I had compiled during my Cancer Treatment. Since I was primarily interested in educating myself about Brain Cancer in general and Glioblastoma Multiform (GBM) in particular, all the notes I have compiled are inclined towards GBM. However, by no means they are specific to GBM. The tips prescribed are not only meant for any bodily disease, but for general well-being and healthy living as well.

Treatment

Healing is a matter of time,
But is sometimes also a matter of opportunity.
-Hippocrates

Brain Cancer for various complexities, is relatively a lesser researched condition in the world, hence ironically the effective treatment is lagging by far. There are several reasons for that, and the main reason is that the Cancer never got the spotlight from the researchers and scientists until the middle of 20th century and now in the 21st century, it is gaining pace. Now, tremendous efforts are being made all over to the world to fully control this beast and give treatment options to patients. It is hard to say whether the brain cancer treatment will have success at par with other types of cancers, but hopes are certainly being directed in that direction. But unfortunately, limitations are real and several, which is the main reason that not significant success rates could be achieved in past 25 years of research.

Current Limitations

So far, the identified limitations are:

New and unknown causes: As our lifestyles change in the 21st century, the new gadgets, new radiations are affecting our bodies and yet we have no clue how exactly. We know that WiFi, Mobile phones, satellite signals etc. all contribute to health hazards, but life seem impossible without them now. They have become necessities of modern living. On top of that environmental issues such as pollution and toxins all around us are worsening the situation by many folds.

Enormous Complexity of human body, where all organs are not only different but incredibly complex in their own built, especially the brain. On top of that all humans have variations in their DNAs and genes, that make the task of finding a common solution almost impossible. This factor, along with the 'new and unknown causes', mentioned above have made it impossible to find out the root cause of cancer in each patient.

Technology in medical science: Though lots of progress is being made in medical research to come up with more effective drugs and also in engineering streams to come with more sophisticated technologies to facilitate the medical research, but still things are not there where they should be. The field of 'biomedical engineering' is *the future* where professionals qualified in medicine and engineering principles would be able to offer more breakthroughs and more rapidly.

Solutions are costly: Whatever treatment is available; it does not come cheap by any means. In UK, the system of NHS supports the patients for free but otherwise the private treatment everywhere in the world, including the UK is extremely pricey. Once a person gets into the spate of any such illness, the health insurance skyrockets as well. Some of the radiotherapy machines, that are capable of providing accurate treatment, cost up to millions of dollars and if they need to be installed closer to the patients, the costs of installations could easily run into billions.

Understanding in Patients: Now that it is spreading like an epidemic, more and more people have now started to understand the Cancer, which is very good. Else, till now, people did not have much clue about this disease except in a very small and closed medical community. Now, the key terms of cancer such as types of cancers, their severity and their basic treatments such as radiotherapy and chemotherapy are being widely understood. Even though the repercussions of less healthy food are still to convince the masses (e.g., meals full of hydrogenated fat or excessive sugars), but fortunately, awareness of nutritious and organic eating is growing as well.

Red Tape-ism: Most of the researches are being conducted under the Government initiatives and funded either by the governments or big pharmaceutical companies. Given the expensive research and development of the cancer drugs, the budgets are not that easy to approve. On top of that the drugs, even if they are made eligible to the cancer patients are tested for several years, if not decades. This time lag hardly motivates any government or a pharma company to invest into R&D. Last but not least, the drug approval processes are unfortunately extremely cumbersome, even though they have been deliberately tailored as such for the benefit of the patients only. For example, even in the most advanced country, USA, it is not easy to get approval of the trials of new solution from FDA (Food and Drug Administration), because their threshold criteria are just too high.

Research in Synergy with Nature: At very basic level, the root cause of cancer is the abnormality induced in the normal functioning of human body. In other words, something has gone wrong in nature as far as the body is concerned. If we take a view that remedy is also available in nature somewhere, then the research could be made lot easier. Thankfully, the research and scientific community has started to widely recognise this fact and the solution is being sought either within body's own immune system or in the 'mother nature'.

Solutions

When we talk of treatment in Cancer, we generally refer to two categories of treatments: Current available Treatments, also called as Traditional Treatments and Future Treatments that are currently under research.

Before I state case of the current stage of treatments or the researches being carried out for the future solutions, let's take a look at the Drug Trial process for the cancer treatment.

The Drug Trials

All cancer drugs are tested thoroughly before they are given to the cancer patients. Typically, this testing is performed in extremely challenging and lengthy phases called 'Clinical Trials' and it's a norm across all countries. Generally, there are 3 phases of trials that are performed on drugs before they get any chance of approval from the designated agencies of the respective country.

After the drug has been tested in laboratories on animals and the chemists are convinced that the drug could be effective, it is then tried on cancer patients, by performing increasingly rigorous trials of the drug.

Phase 1: The proposed drug is first tried on a very small number of volunteer patients; between 10-30 in relatively small dosage, patients suffering from the particular cancer that the drug primarily claims to remediate. Then the drug and its effects on patients are monitored closely by the doctors, including the side effects of the drug. After the trial of up to a year, the oncologists give their verdict on the efficacy of the drug by checking the results that the drug has generated. Only if the drug demonstrates some viable results to the monitoring agencies, the drug is allowed to proceed to the next phase of the trials. Another big hurdle in this phase is to have 10-30 cancer patients for a 'particular cancer' type. For example, how many GBM patients could be found in or around one research centre at a given time? A number of 10 itself looks so improbable and a number 30 definitely seem an extremely challenging task for the trials team. The only slight possibility of finding such as number of patients is in big cities with huge populations.

Phase 2: In the next phase, the drug and its effects are monitored more closely by the doctors and an estimate of correct dosage is formed. Usually, to perform a closer study of the drug, both the volunteer population and the trial period are doubled compared to Phase 1 trials: for example, 20-60 patients and 1-2 years respectively. The safety assessment that was performed during Phase 1 trials is validated. An example could be anti-nausea drugs that were given to the patients during the phase 1 trials. The trials are performed more systematically i.e., the observations are carefully noted down to carry ahead in the most critical phase 3 of the trials. A new concept that is introduced in this phase is called 'randomised' trials. Here patients are selected at random into two groups; one group is assigned to new clinically trials and the second is assigned to the regular and approved treatment. After the trials, if the new treatment shows better results or at least at par with the established treatment, only then the new treatment is given a go ahead for the next and final phase; Phase 3. Clearly, an obvious challenge is worse than the Phase 1 trials i.e., to have a trial population of 30-60 patients for a specific cancer type at a given time. For brain cancers and GBM in particular, it becomes an enormous challenge.

Phase 3: This is the most critical phase of the trials. Not many treatments that go to Phase 2 trials mange to make into Phase 3. But once they are in, then must satisfy the toughest criteria set by the approval agency or agencies. The following are the salient features of Phase 3 trials:

A much larger population of patients is given trials of the treatment and typically the population can run into thousands of patients. This is clearly is not an easy task to identity the patients for a particular cancer and certainly a kind of impossibility for GBM.

- The treatment is tested on different types of cancers and not just the cancer for which it was proposed early on i.e., before Phase 1 trials.

- This phase also contains a great mix of population on the basis of age groups and ethnicity, which is again a big challenge in case the trials are being carried out for a specific type of cancer, and GBM being the worst, because of its rarity.

- The Phase include the culmination of 'multiple proposed drugs', that had conducted their own independent Phase 2 trials, and all drugs are compared to best available standard treatment.

- The trials could last for much longer time and generally across many years and potentially decades, which clearly does not favour the cancer patients in general and GBM patients in particular undergoing these trials.

Given the complexity of the trials across multiple dimensions mentioned above, all the planning and monitoring is performed with the aid of computers, especially in Phase 3. The computers then run a sophisticated software to check the efficacy of the treatments compared to the standard drug on particular types of cancers that exist today (of over 200 known types). Furthermore, the strict criteria set by the drug approval agencies of the country must also be adhered to.

Only after demonstrating the better or at par results with the currently approved drugs, with lesser and controllable side effects to the patients, the treatment is submitted for approval to the approving agency such as FDA in USA or EMA (European Medical Agency) in Europe. The procedure is even tougher in the UK because the proposed drug first has to get an approval from EMA and then UK's own MHRA (The Medicines and Healthcare products Regulatory Agency).

Summary: The irony is that after so many trials and such a long wait, potentially for years, the trials could only get approval, if they get approval at all, for only a specific type of cancer and not for all others. Talking of GBM in particular, almost all of the trials no wonder fails to demonstrate any positive impact on GBM patients. That's how complex our brains and the drug trials are!

Current Treatments

Currently, the 'typical' treatment of the Brain Tumours is performed in three stages – Surgery, Chemotherapy and Radiotherapy. This has been the case from at least last 3 decades.

Surgery

After the diagnosis of Brain Tumour, the first step is to remove the tumour surgically as much as possible. This is called 'de-bulking' of the tumour. The surgical procedure of cutting the skin and skull to access the brain tumour is called 'Craniotomy'. Given the sensitivity of the brain, the de-bulking is a highly complicated procedure making the neurosurgery the most complex field of medical science and at the same time, attracting best surgeons into this domain.

Given the extreme sensitivity and frailty of the brain, should the knife of a neurosurgeon miss the mark even by a millimetre, it could paralyse the patient and cause irreversible damage. A little more error could become a matter of life or death for the patient. But generally, the neurosurgeons are most talented in the field of medical science; they perform craniotomy with extreme accuracy almost never jeopardise the patient's life. And a downside of that is that generally not all of the tumour can be removed during the surgery. It is a question of quality of life after surgery. Also, in spite of the best efforts by a neurosurgeon, some minor but lifelong disabilities still stay with the patients though. As an example, I recovered completely from the surgery and the paralysis that craniotomy gave to me, but I still carry 'papilledema[18]' (also called optical disc swelling) in my right eye and have almost no clear vision and rely on just the left eye for all my work, including typing this book on my computer.

However, the saga for the patient continues even after the surgery and the wound of surgery must be healed with great caution. It must be cleansed at regular intervals and

[18]During the surgery if the optic nerve comes under pressure, then the sight of the eye gets very blurred. Patient struggles to see anything clearly.

multiple times in a day. The cleansing must be performed in a completely hygienic environment using only the prescribed ointments/lotions by the neurosurgeon; completely isolated from any dust or heat. The caregiver of the patient must learn from the nurse how to keep the wound hygienic and how to apply dressings very gently, because any infection on the wound could turn into a disaster for the patient. The hospital nurse can take care of the patient only in the hospital, but once the patient arrives at home, it is the caregiver who assumes the responsibilities of the nurse.

During the first few days of surgery, while the wounds heal, the patients also need to take lots of precautions such as: keep the skull covered all the time including during the sleep time; must notify the nurse or caregiver should the wound makes him/her uncomfortable; not be too adventurous to move and stay absolutely calm physically, mentally and also emotionally.

This can be a testing time not only for the patient and the caregiver but for the whole family around him/her. Finally, the patient and the caretaker need to be regular with the medication prescribed by the neurosurgeon, especially the medicines that heal the surgery and preventive medication for fits or seizures.

Radiotherapy

As mentioned above, often due to hyper-sensitivity of the brain and the severe impact of aggressive surgery on the quality of life, it is not possible to de-bulk the whole tumour. Some of the remaining tumour that is in vicinity with the other vital parts of the brain and head, such as spinal cord and vessels connecting to the sensory organs, has to be left untouched, for the sake of the patient's greater wellbeing.

Once the wounds of the patient heal, the next step is radiotherapy, where in a secure chamber, strong beams are focused on the target i.e., the remnants of tumour to destroy it further. Every effort is made to protect the healthy part (cells and tissues) of the brain. The beams deployed could be of several types and x-ray (Photon) beam being most popular. The others and immensely costlier ones could be based on electron beams, proton beams and gamma beams.

Even though the radiotherapy claims to target only the tumour and not the healthy parts of the body or the organ, but in reality, it's not that simple. The beams after all travel through the healthy tissues before they hit the designated spot of the tumour. En-route, these beams end up in impacting the healthy tissues as well and leave patients suffer from side effects. Of these prominent ones are – burning of skull skin, tiredness and fatigue, swelling of the brain called 'edema', worsening of symptoms especially the cognitive faculties and general sickness. But fortunately, these side effects do not last long, and patient's health is usually restored in weeks; moreover, the radiology-oncologists are also capable of controlling many side effects.

Before the treatment starts, a mask or helmet is custom made for each patient and when the radiation if given, it is very essential that the target in the tumour organ, e.g., the head stays stationary. To stabilize the organ, say brain, the mask is put on the head tightly bolted with the scan bed.

The mask is so tight that the patient can only breath but cannot move the head even a bit. Only at the end of the treatment, when the mask is removed, the patient is capable of speaking. However, an emergency control switch is given in patient's hand, should s(he) feel any suffocation, nausea or any other unpleasant feeling during the radiation therapy.

The radiotherapy treatment typically lasts for 6-8 weeks and each radiation session is simply called 'session' that lasts for 10 minutes or so. Generally, the radiations are administered on every weekday i.e., Monday to Friday and generally the weekends are for rest for the patient. In spite of that, these five days are enough to overwhelm even the most resilient patient.

When chemo drug is given along with the radiation, it is called chemo-radiotherapy (CRT); and the drug is given to improve the overall result, i.e., finer burning of the tumour.

Finally, to bring down the edema caused by radiation, the radiologist-oncologist generally prescribe steroids such as

Dexamethasone, which can typically last for up to 6 weeks after the radiotherapy treatment ends.

Chemotherapy

Even after radiotherapy, some tiny tumour spots and tumour roots that have penetrated in the brain may become difficult to burn by radiation. The final stage of the treatment is giving highly toxic drugs to the patient with an intention to further destroy the remaining cancer cells. This is the most difficult phase of the treatment for the patient and a real testing time of her/his will power. Even though chemotherapy is given to the patients in order to destroy the tumour cells; however, in reality it is not that simple. Since the drug circulates in the whole body, the drug ends up impacting the healthy part of the body as well, which explains why the bodies of many patients who undergo chemotherapy shrink so much and sometimes, in the extreme cases, even bearing the skeleton of the patient. However, normally, depending upon the drug being given to the patient and its side effects, that the oncologist has to manage.

The following are key chemotherapy drugs that are given to the brain cancer patients:

Temozolomide (TMZ): It is the main drug for the Brain Cancer in general and GBM in particular. The drug is essentially an alkalising agent that combats the acidic tumour and intends to stop the tumour cells from making the DNAs; and eventually to stop its growth; with a final and obvious goal of eliminating the tumour altogether.

Usually, the treatment runs for 6 monthly cycles and in each cycle, for a week, the patient has to take prescribed number of capsules. They are not allowed to eat anything for two hours before and after taking the drug. This protocol is simple to mention, but in reality, it can come with a wide range of symptoms.

Even though TMZ is considered as a 'gold standard' chemo drug in the medical community, unfortunately, this drug does not suit everyone and in cases it has failed. This happened to me as well and my oncologist had to resort to a 'cocktail' of other chemo drugs when TMZ was proven to be ineffective.

Lomustine: This drug is another alkalising agent just like TMZ but differs in the manner how it stops the cancer cell DNA from spreading. But the final goal of both the drugs is the same; first to stop the tumour from growing and then aim to eliminate it altogether.

Usually, it is given as a single dose (single capsule) that the patient has to take after every 4-6 weeks or as prescribed by the oncologist.

Lomustine is a simpler name for the real drug name of CCNU, where CCNU stands for a chemical formula of the drug i.e., 1-(2-Chloroethyl)-3-Cyclohexyl-1-NitrosoUrea.

Procarbazine: This drug is bit different from the TMZ and Lomustine described above. First, the drug is classified as 'cytotoxin', i.e., generates toxicity for the cancer cells. Second, it was primarily developed for other cancers such as Hodgkin lymphoma (cancer of white blood cells) and that too amongst children. Later it was used to treat lower grades of brain cancers, other than the GBM. Another aspect is that it is hardly given alone for the Brain Cancers and is generally given with Lomustine to be effective.

Vincristine: Vincristine is yet another drug that is primarily used for other cancers and seem to be working on the Brain Cancers as well. The drug works by stopping the cancer cells from dividing thereby stopping the spread of the cancer. This characteristic is called anti-mitotic, where 'mitosis' means cell division.

Vincristine is administered intravenously by putting a drip. When I got my Vincristine dose, I was told that the drug is most effective when freshly prepared and has a short shelf life.

Note: During my chemotherapy treatment that lasted almost a year, I was first given TMZ for 3 months. When my oncologist discovered that the drug did not produce any positive result, he switched to the cocktail of PVC (Procarbazine, Vincristine and CCNU/Lomustine). PVC too jolted my body enormously, but eventually, it did lead to positive scans.

Side Effects

The following are the typical side effects of almost all of the chemotherapy drugs. The chemo drug does not only cause direct side-effects, rather the drug works in an uncanny and in-direct manner as well, by destroying the immunity of the body first and then it is the weak body that gives up to the onslaught of the toxic drug, eventually producing more of these side-effects.

These side-effects of the chemotherapy could be listed as below:

Extreme Nausea: Depending upon the dosage of the chemo drug, the patient is likely to suffer from nausea. This is logical as well. As the chemo drug spreads toxicity in the patient's body, it tends to kill all cells that come in its way; even though the intention is to destroy only the cancer cells.

As the body's immune system crumbles, the patient's health start to suffer as well. The nausea triggers repulsion of food because whatever the patient consumes, s(he) throws it out. This generally results in the emaciation of the body.

The way to confront nausea is to take anti-nausea drugs that the oncologist has prescribed and eat food at a very slow pace, and preferably dry food. Also, the patient needs to carefully monitor the response of the body and stop at the right time when the body starts to show first sign of any reaction to the food intake. When I used to suffer during my chemotherapy, I used to eat dry wholemeal toast along with herbal tea, at an extremely slow pace. Sometimes to finish just one toast and a cup of herbal tea, I would spend a complete hour. Secondly, there is something in onion, garlic, ginger and other root ingredients that kills the nausea. I would strongly advise to everyone, patient or no patient, to eat garlic and ginger as much as you can and if you don't find them appealing, you could always alternate the recipe to disguise the taste of these most vital ingredients.

Damaged Skin: It would be too naïve to think that the chemotherapy affects the patient only from inside and spares the body from outside. But that is certainly not the case. Chemotherapy is perfectly capable of damaging the skin and it does. There were many nights during my treatment when the only reason for not getting even a wink of sleep during the night, was itch on my skin caused by fissures that the chemo drug had given all over the body. I used the combination process of treating the skin with calamine lotion and removing the dryness with almond oil. It must continue as long as the patient is taking the chemo drugs; and even beyond that till the skin recovers completely. Moreover, the patient must be ready to accept the fact that the skin sensitivity to external environment factors such as heat and pollution might be permanent.

Drop in Immunity: Last but not least, since the chemotherapy toxicity destroys the healthy body cells, it eventually damages the immunity of the patient against every external agent and the body becomes susceptible to infections and allergies. Infections such as cold and flu during the seasonal change; and allergies such allergies such as from dust, pollution, pollens or even scents. That's the reason that the patients usually switch to organic and natural toiletries during the treatment and keep their respiratory system protected when out of the hygienic environment. In order to counteract the drop in immunity, the patient and the caregiver must make every effort to keep the surroundings absolutely clean, fresh and dust free. And to maintain the general strength of the body, good nutrition becomes very important; including consumption all foods that are rich in iron such as spinach, broccoli and many lentils. Because the food intake during this period is limited, it is vital to ensure every mouthful is packed with nutrition.

I can't stress this enough - absolute care is must during the change of season. This happened to me when I got terrible chest infection during the penultimate cycle of chemotherapy. To fix the infection, I had no option but to take a course of strong anti-biotic, that further dropped the platelet counts and ultimately leading to the delay in the final cycle of treatment with two months lost before my blood tests revived to acceptable levels and I was permitted to take last dose of chemo drug. During these two months, my only aim was to raise the iron levels in the blood and I was surviving only on spinach soup with ginger, garlic, turmeric and sometimes spirulina as additional ingredients. It is easier to say than done, but in this particular case, the patient and the caregiver must remember – 'Prevention is far better than cure'.

The future of non-invasive treatment

Most of the treatments that are being investigated now in labs or trial runs are based on two broad categories – 'Immunotherapy' and 'Virotherapy'. There is a great enthusiasm in the medical community for both of these approaches because both the treatments offer non-invasive approach (without performing any surgery on the patient's skull) to the Brain Cancer. Also, it is being hoped that these approaches will be much better than the conventional treatment and hopefully will add many years to patient's life and with lesser side effects.

Immunotherapy

In immunotherapy approach, the immunity of the body is given a big boost. This is based on premise that our bodies are capable of dealing with any infections, including early cancer like distortions, that are triggered by the foreign agents such as bacteria or viruses. Since the immune system and cancer are both part of the same body, another underlying cause of cancer is the failure of body's immune system to identify that the cancer cells as harmful to the body and by not acknowledging the need to destroy them. In immunotherapy, the approach is to enhance the body's immune system further to identify the trickster cancer cells as enemies rather than friends. Once the patient gets a dose of the immunotherapy drug, the body starts to work automatically and begins to destroy the cancer cells.

However, the key challenge in this approach is to determine precisely *how much* immunity needs to be enhanced for the patient in order to target his/her tumour. Moreover, since the dosage is likely to be different for every patient, it means there probably won't be any standard dosage for all the patients. Thirdly, the process generally includes taking out body's healthy cells, enhancing them to fight cancer and then injecting back in the body to fight and destroy the cancer cells. This is an enormously complex process that needs not only painfully high precision but also absolutely careful handling of the process in order to avoid any contamination.

There are some of the FDA approved medicines that fall under Immunotherapy regime and are currently being used at places. For example:

Avastin: The real medicinal name is Bevacizumab, is a cancer medicine that interrupts the growth of the cancer cells, including in the brain. Generally, it is given intravenously for all other cancers and for brain cancer patients it is injected directly into the brain tumour bypassing the blood-brain barrier. FDA approved this treatment in the USA in year 2012 for the 'reoccurring' GBMs as it had demonstrated shrinking of the tumour. But the European approval agencies took a different position. Their understanding was that the drug was shrinking the 'swelling' inside and around the tumour and not the tumour per se. That made Europe, including the UK, reject the medicine as not a proven cure to the GBM. Instead, UK began to do trial runs of Bevacizumab (Avastin) along with a new drug called Dasatinib (sold under the brand name Sprycel). At the time of writing of this text in April 2018, the trial runs had not concluded anything.

Further in April 2021, The Institute of Cancer Research in London, reported[19]:

"Two of the first 10 patients treated for a highly aggressive type of brain cancer called glioblastoma responded to the immunotherapy agent atezolizumab when combined with ipatasertib, a new precision drug that may be able to uncloak tumours to the immune system."

Clearly, to the frustrations of patients of the GBM Cancer, this is a sign of progress but still not any magic wand. Clearly, that only shows the complexity of the disease rather than anything else. Still, this is a space worth watching closely in future.

CAR-T: Amongst the several cells in our immune system, one of the cells is named as T cells.

All chemical substances that do not originate within the body have certain proteins on the surface of their cells, called **antigens**. On the other hand, body's own immune cells such as T-cells, have their own proteins, called **receptors** that *attach* to foreign antigens and help trigger

---

19 https://www.icr.ac.uk/news-archive/immunotherapy-combination-shows-early-promise-in-aggressive-brain-cancers

other parts of the immune system to destroy the foreign substance i.e., the antigens. The cancer cells also have antigens but having developed in the same environment as the T-cells, they have tendency not be noticed by the immune cells including of course the T-cells. In CAR-T therapy, these T-cells are extracted out of the patient's body, *synthetically* enhanced, and are then injected back in the body with an intention to boost up the immune system and with an eventual aim to identify and destroy the cancer cells of the tumour. These artificially enhanced T cells outside the body are called the CAR-T cells, where CAR stands for 'Chimeric Antigen Receptor', and 'chimeric' simply means 'having parts from different origin'. But it is sufficient to know that CAR-T cells are *synthetically altered* T cells outside the patient's body.

The treatment is however being developed as it is facing lots of challenges. The primary challenge is - as the CAR-T cells start to multiply in the body, because of having components with their origins outside the body's DNA, they start to give severe side effects such as very high fevers and dangerously low blood pressures, nausea etc. At moment, the doctors are finding ways to manage these side effects. Just like Avastin therapy, this therapy is also worth watching. This therapy was tried in vain to treat Senator John McCain, in August 20018, in the USA – but we lost him within months after the diagnosis of GBM. Still, it is worth tracking news on this treatment, as I am sure that Oncologists and the other medicine professions, including in the pharmaceutical industry, must have taken some lessons after Senator McCain passed away and shall aim to refine the treatment further.

Virotherapy

Virotherapy takes the entirely different approach to immunotherapy. Whereas in immunotherapy, the reliance is on using or enhancing the immune system of the body, in Virotherapy on the other hand, specific viruses are deliberately injected into the body with an intention to destroy the cancer/tumour cells only. This is clearly an anti-thesis of immunotherapy because we are *infecting* the body on purpose; with a hope to work *against* the immune system of the body to achieve our objective of destroying the cancer. Moreover, since it is the virus that is being injected into the body, it has a potential of damaging or infecting the body itself. For example, doesn't injecting of polio virus in the body seem a scary thought at first instance? But the scientists have been seeing the advantages of using the viruses to destroy cancer cells over the disadvantages of the side effects of the injected virus, which they have been trying to control since last 40 years or so. Now, with the advancements of medicinal research and instrumentation engineering, there is a renewed interest in this approach and scientists have faith that the Virotherapy can be used to specifically to target the cancer/tumour cells without going closer to the normal or healthy cells.

All this is being made possible with new inventions such as 'hair -thin syringes' that can administer the medicine in extremely localised area, equal to a diameter of a hair, to deliver the medicine. Though this kind of treatment has not been given to patients as yet, but it is being given very high priority and attention in the medicinal research, especially the prospects of delivering the drug deep inside the brain and blood vessels; given the ability to penetrate right up to centre of the brain where with current invasive technology is almost impossible to reach, without putting the patient at big risk. Not only the technology of making hair thin syringe needle, but also there is an issue of automatically calculating the right amount of dosage that need to be injected into the tumour. This further demand that the 'hair thin' needle tip also need to have a sensor to detect the tumour area where the medicine is being dripped and then send the information back to the injecting mechanism outside the patients' body; that will further regulate how much further dosage is required.

In spite of all these current limitations, there is an increasing enthusiasm in the medical community and the final product is not too far for the clinical trials on humans. My personal understanding is that we are not too far from this breakthrough – we are not talking of decades of wait but hopefully much lesser. At the time of writing this text in early 2018, my understanding was confirmed by none other than the research department of MIT, in the USA[20].

Future of Radiations

---

[20] https://www.statnews.com/2018/01/24/implant-brain-remote-control/

As the name suggests, Radiotherapy implies Radiation driven therapy, where strong radiations are given to the tumours in order to destroy cancerous or malignant cells. The radiation beam is accelerated before it targets the tumour, and this acceleration is achieved in what is called 'Liner Accelerator', or simply LINAC.

There are different types of radiation therapies and they all have their pros and cons. The oncologist of the patient determines what radiation is to be given to the patient, which is further driven by the fact what radiation facilities are available to the oncologist. Nevertheless, the patient must be conversant with these different types so that the treatment could be understood and to appreciate the progress being made in this field.

With the arrival of the CT and MRI Scan facilities, these radiation techniques have got a tremendous boost. This is because the CT and MRI can perform a 3D imaging of the tumour and the radiation machines can effectively provide radiations from different angles or from all directions. Another advantage is that since the radiations are specifically targeted at the tumours, they do minimal harm to the healthy organs that comes in their way. For example, if radiation is to be given to a brain tumour then the beam could be directly focused on the tumour and important organs such as spinal cord could be protected. At moment, there is still not much accuracy in the machine, but the enhancements are being worked upon. In future as the advanced versions of these technologies and systems emerge, it is not that the healthy organs will not be exposed to the radiations; they certain will be, but the impact will be absolute minimal and easily remediable.

Type of Radiation Therapies

The various types of Radiotherapies can be summarised as below:

IMRT: Intensity Modulated Radio Therapy - As the name suggests it is a method of radiation delivery using beams of varying 'intensities' to closely fit the area of cancer. The radiations are varied with a special inbuilt device called 'multi leaf collimator[21]', which is made of thin leaves (of lead) and move independently, thus controlling the

---

[21]Collimator - a device or part of the machine that narrows the radiation bean.

radiation to the precise target area of the tumour, while protecting nearby healthy cells and organs.

VMAT: Volumetric Modulated Arc Therapy is bit advanced compared to IMRT in terms of precision of both the intensity control and the area control. As the name suggests, the unique characteristic of this approach is 'volumetric', 'modulated' and 'arc'. Volumetric implies 'volume' or concentration of beams at designated spot, 'modulated' means that the intensity of the beam could be regulated, and 'Arc' implies that the radiation machine's 'beam collimator' can rotate to effectively give radiation from multiple dimensions. Another big advantage of this therapy over IMTR is that the patient is exposed to radiations for a very short duration that typically runs in seconds and not in minutes. RapidArc™, is one such example of VMAT that is used to many types of tumours including the brain tumour.

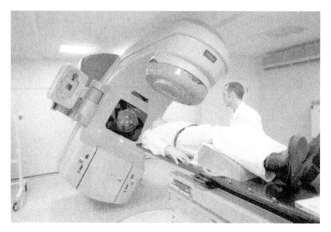

Fig. 3 : Source: https://blogit.realwire.com/media/IMG_3810.jpg

SRS: Stereotactic[22] Radiosurgery works on the same principle as outlined above in IMRT and VMAT of focussing the radiation on the tumour. Stereotactic radiosurgery (SRS) is a highly precise form of radiation therapy initially developed to treat small brain tumours and functional abnormalities of the brain. The principles of cranial SRS, namely high precision radiation where delivery is accurate to within one to two millimetres is getting much deserved attention of the radiologists. Despite its name, SRS is a non-surgical procedure that delivers precisely targeted radiation at much higher doses, in only a single or few treatments, as compared to traditional radiation

---

[22]Stereotactic - pertaining to types of brain surgery that use a system of three-dimensional coordinates to locate the site to be operated on.

therapy. This treatment is only possible due to the development of highly advanced radiation technologies that permit maximum dose delivery within the target while minimizing dose to the surrounding healthy tissue. The goal is to deliver doses that will destroy the tumour and achieve permanent local control. SRS is typically used for Brain and Spine Tumours. Due to complexity in operations, the task is usually achieved when the radiology oncologist and neurosurgeon work together.

SBTR: The version that is used to treat other body parts besides the brain, is called SBRT or Stereotactic 'Body' Radiation Therapy. SBTR is also called SABR i.e., Stereotactic ablative[23] radiotherapy.

SRS and SBRT rely on several technologies:

- three-dimensional imaging and localization techniques that determine the exact coordinates of the target within the body.
- systems to immobilize and carefully position the patient and maintain the patient position during therapy

---

[23]Ablative – to just erode away [the Tumour] with radiation.

- highly focused gamma-ray or x-ray beams that converge on a tumour or abnormality

- image-guided radiation therapy (IGRT) which uses medical imaging to confirm the location of a tumour immediately before, and in some cases, during the delivery of radiation. IGRT improves the precision and accuracy of the treatment.

SRS and SBRT are important alternatives to invasive surgery, especially for patients who are unable to undergo surgery and for tumours and abnormalities that are:

- hard to reach

- located close to vital organs/anatomic regions

- subject to movement within the body

Beam Types

The beams that are radiated from the collimator are of several types. Though they all serve the same purpose of burning the tumour, but still there are some differences, and these differences will be highlighted in the subsequent, dedicated sections below.

At the high level, the categorization of the beam types is as follows:

- *Conventional Beams* (X-Ray/Photon Beams).
- *Proton Beams*
- *Gamma Rays*

X-Ray Beams: These are the conventional beams used in most of the radiotherapy treatments and is sometimes called as *Photon Beams* as well. By default, the installation of the radiotherapy always implies the X-Ray(Photon) beam. Generally, all the beam types serve one purpose and that is to damage the DNA of the cancer cells, by collating strong beam of accelerated photons on the tumour. Alternatively, the beams could create the unstable charged particles called 'free radicles'[24] and they in turn can destroy the DNAs and stabilising themselves. Whichever way the DNAs of the cancer cells are damaged, the results are the same: the cancer cells begin to die and eventually flushed out of the body as 'waste'. It's not that the healthy cells do

---

[24]Oxygen in the body splits into single atoms with unpaired electrons. Electrons like to be in pairs, so these atoms, called free radicals, scavenge the body to seek out other electrons so they can become a pair. This causes damage to cells, proteins and DNA. Source - http://www.healthchecksystems.com/antioxid.htm

not get damaged during the process, in fact they do, but they get repaired or replaced easily. During the process, should any side effects occur, the radiologist oncologist is perfectly capable of handling or remediating them.

The beams that are delivered to the cancer cells are precise and focused. Every effort is made by the team to keep the normal tissues safe.

Sometimes the radiation is also given in small doses and these small doses are called *fractions*. There are two reasons why the dose is split into fractions, First, not all patients are strong enough to bear the brunt of full dose and in those cases the radiations are given piecemeal, hence in fractions. Second, the radiations could result in giving side effects such as pains in some part of the patient's body, and fractions could be applied in those parts to alleviate the pains.

Lastly, since the session typically last for maximum of half an hour, the patient may go for radiation every day, like I did. Some elderly patients however, who live at farther distances from the hospital facilities, opt to stay in the hospital throughout the treatment.

Proton Beams: The most fundamental principle of Proton bean therapy is same as the Photon bean therapy explained above, i.e., focusing high intensity radiations on tumour while protecting the healthy areas around the tumour untouched. However, in practical aspects, there are some significant differences between these two beams:

1) Irrespective of the depth of the tumour in the body, the traditional beams strike at the surface of the organ at full intensity. The proton beam on the other hand could be controlled in such a manner that at the surface, the beam is less intense yet unleashes its full power at the target that is lying much deeper. This spot where the photon beam reaches its highest intensity is called 'Bragg Peak' and is demonstrated in the figure below.

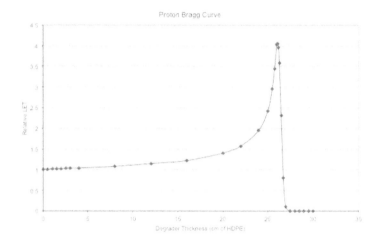

Fig. 4 : Source : https://www.bnl.gov/nsrl/userguide/bragg-curves-and-peaks.php

The Bragg Peak makes proton beams are more precise compare to the Photon Beams in targeting the affected areas.

2) The higher precision implies more sparing of the healthy tissues.

3) More sparing of healthy tissues further implies lesser side-effects of radiotherapy to the patient. For example, if a patient loses all of his/her hair during the conventional therapy, then this loss will be localised or much less under the Proton Beam radiation.

4) Before the Proton Radiations enter the body of the patient, it goes through last component of the therapy system called 'compensator', which is capable of providing finer level of focussing of the beam to the target i.e., the tumour.

In spite of all these obvious benefits the proton beam therapy has its limitations as well, making it less feasible to make available to all the needy patients. There are:

1) The size of the whole therapy system is a biggest constraint. The typical machine and its related systems such as LINAC typically have dimensions of football field size and height equivalent to 3 story building. This factor alone makes the system for the treatment a rarity and makes the whole infrastructure and its treatment extremely expensive.

2) The Proton beam no doubt is capable of targeting the specific area but in reality, this feature is only available in the high-end machines generating finer proton beam called 'scanning beam', which is capable of delivering finer 'Bragg

Peak' and at the same time capable to going much deeper into the tumour as well.

Unfortunately, due to the limitations listed above, these kinds of sophisticated systems are not widely available yet.

Gamma Knife Surgery

Gamma Knife Surgery (GKS), as the name suggests is an alternative to invasive surgery, Craniotomy, that most GBM patients have to go through. In GKS, no surgical procedure takes place and 'small' tumours could be destroyed with the precisely focused high intensity gamma rays. Since no incision is involved, it is a type of 'Stereotactic Radio Surgery' (SRS).

In SRS, approximately 200 beams of low intensity of gamma rays are focused on the tumour from several directions. Even though each beam is low in intensity, but by the time all these beams converge on the target spot, the concentration becomes very potent and is well capable of burning the tumour cells. This also implies that the normal tissues through which the individual beams travel stay 'almost' untouched.

GKS is primarily used to treat Brain Tumours and for other cancers, as mentioned earlier, a slightly different machine is used called SBRT (Stereotactic Body Radiation Therapy).

Needless to say, the highly concentrated beam on the tumour implies that the tumour spot must be held absolutely static. To achieve the immobility of the patient's head, a special helmet is used to keep the patient's skull tight. Due to its very hi-tech engineering that includes a built-in nuclear reactor to deliver the gamma rays, the helmet is enormously costly.

The figure below shows how a typical helmet infrastructure of GKS looks like.

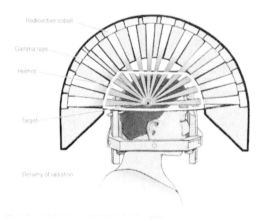

Fig. 5 : Source : https://www.mayoclinic.org/-/media/kcms/gbs/patient-consumer/images/2015/03/10/09/58/mcdc7_gamma_knife_headframe-8col.jpg

The radioactive (nuclear) gamma rays are generated by the 'radioactive cobalt' area and the beams are finely targeted to spot in the target which is very small with a maximum diameter of 2.5 cm. To achieve this high accuracy, the patient's skull is tied very firmly using the bolts in the helmet, that puts patient's strength and patience to test.

Treatment Dosage: The typical treatment of GKS lasts from few days to several months, depending upon the malignancy of the cancer. During the treatment, the patient undergoes the session every day and each session lasts between 45 minutes to up to a couple of hours, again, depending upon the tumour, its size and malignancy.

Side Effects: The gamma radiations though are effective in burning the tumour, but given their strength, they too give side effects to the patient. Some of the commonly known side effects are:

- Pain and tenderness where the screws or pins were placed.
- Nausea and vomiting.
- Dizziness.
- Headaches.
- Hair loss where the radiation was directed.
- Damage to surrounding tissues in the brain, caused by swelling. These effects may be delayed and may cause symptoms mimicking a stroke or a recurrence of tumour.

Limitations: In spite of the best treatment available to deal with Brain Tumours, especially the GBM, the GKS is not without its own limitations, which are:

1) The treatment is effective if the Brain Tumour is small in size. In other words, if the tumour is diagnosed in the early stages, but it hardly ever happens like that. Generally, the tumours, such as GBM, are diagnosed when they are in their advanced stages and the patient's symptoms start to get too serious to be ignored. In such scenario, once the MRI or CT Scan reveals the tumour, the neurosurgeons hardly have time to wait for the preparation for the non-invasive surgery, even if the facilities are at disposal, and they just opt for surgery on ASAP basis. Their most common and sane argument is that the patient must be given immediate relief by 'de bulking' the tumour, else there is always a risk of fatal stoke.

2) The patient has to undergo many sessions of treatment and with Brain Tumours in general and with GBM in particular, that is the risk that neurosurgeons or the patients do not want to take and just go ahead with Craniotomy.

3) The helmets of the GKS systems are immensely costly, due to ultra-sophisticated technology that includes

nuclear manipulation of the beams. These factors imply that helmets are not only immensely costly to manufacture but they have definitive life span too.

4) At one centre alone, the massive investment (of over $4 million), hardly manages a break-even of the costs involved. This becomes the natural deterrent to both the cancer centre and the patient as a treatment option.

5) GKS is more effective for tumours of small sizes, typically less than 2.5 cm in diameter. For the bigger tumours, i.e., greater than 2.5cm diameter, which most of them are, the oncologists prefer the treatment with conventional radiotherapy anyway.

6) The whole procedure is very time consuming because the burning at one spot at a time is no more than $2mm^2$ of area, which implies several hours of radio-oncologist to treat a patient. For example, to treat a tumour with an average size of $3cm^2$ or $300mm^2$, it will take around 150 sessions of radiations, which is clearly not only a torture for the patient, but clearly for the radiologist-oncologist and the radiographer as well.

Currently all the limitations mentioned above are the big deterrent from using or spreading this technology. But having said that, with the advancement in science and technology, these systems are only going to better and better with time and we can hope for some good breakthroughs in next few years.

Cyber-knife

Cyber-knife is a state of art 'robot driven' radiation therapy, which in principle is similar to Gamma Knife Surgery (GKS) discussed above, yet distinct in many ways. Cyber-knife works with normal Photon based beam and yet is considered as an 'incredible invention' by the medical community. The key feature of the Cyber-knife system is that it is a 'robot' and it manoeuvres with enormous flexibility to deliver its highly precise radiation at an incredibly small spot of the tumour, which is generally 1mm in diameter.

The figure below shows the Cyber-knife system in working.

Fig. 7: Image Copyright – The Royal Marsden Cancer Charity, England

As can be seen, the collimator of the system has a very narrow front, from where the rays are focused. These fronts are further adjustable and their 'apertures' could be varied to the high precision focussing on the tumour spot up to 1mm in diameter. Moreover, the collimator performs the MRI scan automatically as it rotates in all directions, in order to enhance the efficacy of the treatment.

Another benefit is that the patient is in complete resting position. Unlike radiotherapy there are no masks and unlike GKS there are no helmets to give pain. The benefit of this technology is that the collimator is highly precise and keep tracking the tumour spot, even if the patient makes slight movement, for example during breathing. In essence, the system is capable of not only of finely tracking the head movement of the patient and the tumour inside it, but also at the same time burning the same tumour with 1mm precision. No doubt, it is an engineering feat.

Limitations: In spite of an incredible achievement the Cyber-knife suffers the same limitations as GKS.

- It can only operate the GBM tumours that are less than 3.5mm in diameter, even with its widest apertures. Generally, the brain tumours and GBM in particular are much larger than this size, making the de-bulking by incision a necessity. Moreover, if the tumour is still left behind, then burning it further with conventional radiotherapy is more pragmatist approach rather than opting for Cyber-knife. Only the miniscule tumour that is left or should reoccur can be more practically handled with Cyber-knife.

- The cost if the installation, that could run up to $10 million is not justified just for treatment of GBM alone. Of course, the machine can be used to perform stereotactic ablative body radiotherapy (SABR), to treat other forms of tumours in rest of the body, then the investment 'might' possibly give a break-even return of the investment made. Moreover, most of the treatment centres, private or government, need to make some profits as well, which makes heavy investments in such machines not very lucrative investments.

- A high degree of understanding and training is essential and is emphasized before the system is put to use in clinical practice by any centre. The team consisting of radiation oncologists, medical physicists, radiographers and other technologists should fully understand the principle and technological features of the Cyber-knife. Clinicians should understand the tumour biology of short-course treatment with high dose/ fraction; physicists should know the accuracy and dose-delivery principles; and radiographers should know the principles, the accuracy desired and achievable and finally, the consequences of errors and their impact on treatment delivery.

- There has not been much significant improvement in the median survival of GBM patients, in spite of treating patients with Cyber-knife.

In other words, when it comes to practicality, Cyber-knife should be used in the end, even after chemotherapy in order to destroy the residuals of the tumour; or when the tumour just begins to make a comeback and the patients manage to catch the revived symptoms relatively much early.

Summary

As mentioned above, even though the big advancements are being made in the technology to assist in fine refining of the Proton beam therapy, Gamma Surgery and of course Cyber-knife, but evidences clearly show that a lot need to be done if humanity has to wins the race against again cancer in general, and GBM in particular. The way I see all this affair that from last 25 years or so, there has not been much advancement in the treatment of GBM. All countries still rely on 'traditional' treatment of surgery, chemotherapy and radiotherapy.

But all this is going to improvise in a big way in times to come and we don't need to wait for decades, but only in years when much better results for patient's survival rate will be demonstrated. Since the researches are being carried out in almost all nations of the world; as a GBM patient, I hope that in near future, as these efforts to be co-ordinated and the bio-scientists, oncologists and pharma companies all over the world work together in synergy. The epidemic is not restricted to a single country or a continent but is prevalent all over the globe.

Resources

https://www.cancer.org/treatment/treatments-and-side-effects/treatment-types/immunotherapy/car-t-cell1.html

https://www.quora.com/How-is-gamma-knife-surgery-different-than-a-radiotherapy-or-a-radio-surgery
https://www.everydayhealth.com/brain-tumor/gamma-knife-surgery.aspx

Complementary and Alternate Medicines (CAM)

You can't always control what goes on outside,
but you can always control what goes on inside.

- Wayne Dyer

During my treatment, I discovered that there is no doubt the standard medicines and treatments are most critical for the cancer patient, because they are tested and proven in laboratories and the go through immensely challenging approval tests by the national healthcare agencies. All this is to establish the efficacy of drugs and to protect general wellbeing of the cancer patients. Even though it is this fundamental principle of consumer protection at the core of the drug approval agencies, still there is a criticism prevalent, especially by the patients on whom the conventional medicine does not work, of denying them the fundamental right of trying the unproven medicines, even if the patient takes all the risk; and patients and the caretakers make desperate 'last' attempts to have access to the still unapproved therapies. But sadly, due to several reasons, this is causing frustration in all groups involved. Physicians want to play safe while handling a cancer patient and the patient community on the other hand become desperate to explore other avenues particularly as the patient reach the critical or terminal stage of their illness. The debate on this topic is endless and we can only hope that the whole system makes progress to give us more survival rates.

Amidst all this unsettled scenario, there are still many 'options' available that the patient can undertake; of course, in consultation with the oncologist or the physician. By doing that, the patient does not impose the whole burden of the treatment on the medical science, rather share some of that on his/her own shoulders as well and in some manner obtain a degree of control. I have seen that this makes the patient more positive and the physicians get motivated as well, seeing their patients sharing responsibility for their self-healing.

These alternate approaches, which 'might' benefit the patients alongside the mainstream medicine, can be broadly classified into two distinct groups: Complementary Therapies and Alternate Therapies.

Complementary Therapies

The complementary therapies 'complements' the main treatment, or 'enhance' the main treatment, by preparing the patient, physically and mentally, for the onslaught of the very tough drugs protocol of cancer treatments. With complementary therapies, that are completely non-controversial and unobtrusive of the main treatment, the patient feels physically stronger, mentally calmer and spiritually at peace. Few examples of these therapies are: Massage Therapy, Music Therapy, Acupuncture, Meditation, Physiotherapy, Psychotherapy and Aromatherapy.

Massage Therapy is the most harmless and non-controversial complementary therapy. Conditionally, it is done very gently on the patients, especially on the affected areas, it is capable of bringing immense relief to the patient. Obviously, the masseur must be fully trained and on top of that very well conversant with the patients' condition. Generally, the massage is given by some natural oils such as 'sweet almond oil'. With right kind of oil, the body and mind go into relaxation mode and all the worries and anxieties start to disappear. It is very important to keep doing the massage at very frequent interval and ideally every day. If masseur is not available, then the patient or the caregiver have to make an effort to do the essential massage. Doing so, brings immense benefits for the well-being of the patient. Massage not only heals the patient mentally but also physically. In my example, apart from the obvious benefits, the regular massage by 'sweet almond oil' cured and revived my skin that was damaged by the toxic chemo drugs. I was lucky that my mother was a qualified masseur, and she took great care of me during her stay with us. Having said that, every patient must explore way(s) to get healing massage. On looking around, the patient/carer is bound to get one. If not in family or relationships, the doors of charities can certainly be knocked – especially in the bigger cities.

Meditation again is another highly effective, yet non-controversial technique to calm your mind and body. There are many different types of meditations such as spiritual meditation or mantra meditation and patient must pick what suits her. It is essential to first try all sort of meditations. When I tried all these forms, I particularly liked 'mindfulness meditation'. I had bought an audio CD of 'mindfulness meditation' by Mark Williams and would listen to the audio in nights to calm myself till I felt completely drowsy.

Music Therapy: One of my favorite therapies; where patient can listen to very calming and gentle music to relax completely. Even better would be if someone could play gentle music for the patient. I was lucky again that I had St Luke's hospice at a walking distance from my home, where I met with a wonderful and kind musician, Alan Watts. Every Tuesday, I would visit the centre to listen his very gentle and relaxing music. He would play several instruments such a Tibetan Bowls, Harp, Native American Flute, Monochord and last but not least an eight-string guitar. He would play with such serenity that many patients including myself would often drift to 'blissful' sleep in the afternoon. The patient and the caregiver are highly recommended to find such places around them for 'real' and 'therapeutic' music. Alternatively, patient could put the relaxing music on the audio set (or Internet) as well. The key is that the music should be very gentle and like a 'white noise' and best time is when the patient wishes to go to sleep. If patient is doing meditation as well, then the music must be played after the meditation session is over and he/she is ready to drop off to sleep. Gentle music with relaxed breathing also keeps all ill thoughts at bay.

Acupuncture is a traditional Chinese method of healing, where very thin needles are inserted in the key body spots (including in the head) to relive the pain and kill the nausea. However, the key to this is if the therapist can apply tiny needles at the right spot, as the guess work clearly won't be effective at all. I was lucky again that at the same centre, St Luke's hospice, I received a great treatment and my therapist Ruth Bony, who was very talented. The needles no doubt give some twitch, but it was worth it. After a while, when the blood circulates in the body, the patient feels relaxed and all pain disappears. There are several doubts amongst people about the efficacy of this treatment and the tip is that the therapist must be fully aware of the patient's condition and patient must also be honest with the therapist while explaining the illness and the treatment pains and help her in identifying the body parts where cure is needed.

Psychotherapy: Of all the complementary therapies, this treatment provides a gold plating over everything else. One of the main factors that cancer develops is when human body is under *stress*, not only physically but also mentally and emotionally. It becomes absolutely essential for the patient to take psychotherapy to alleviate the stresses, tensions and worries. These negativities just disappear when we discuss our burdens with someone, especially a qualified therapist. An intelligent therapist knows how to extract the trapped emotions out of their patients. Just like music therapy, I was fortunate to get some psychotherapy from a Joanne Reinelt, a very talented hypnotherapist in London. Even though I took therapy from her before I was diagnosed with the illness, but during the treatment I would replay her instructions in my mind and reading books on the same subject to reinforce Joanne's guiding tips. With the help of psychotherapy, I could 'untangle' all my thoughts and had started to think clearly.

Physiotherapy: Last but not least, any form of gentle physical exercise is must for a patient such as a walk in a park or in a fresh air. Along with the walks, I decided to do gardening and the blossoming flowers would bring immense tranquility to my mind and spirit.

But in order to alleviate stiffness caused by toxic drugs, nothing beats gentle physiotherapy if given by a caring therapist. Again, just like acupuncture therapist, the physiotherapist also must be fully aware of the patient's condition and patient must also give correct information to the therapist, so that appropriate exercises could be charted out for the patient. It was mainly due to very good physiotherapy that I received at two occasions that I managed to restore my physical health to some degree.

Summary: The key message on the complementary therapies is that they are completely harmless as they do not disrupt the main treatment that the patient receives. Rather, they *complete* the treatment in many ways. Even though no oncologist should have any objection but still it is advisable that the patient must consult the oncologist prior to resuming any therapy and 'sincerely' give regular feedback about the results to the therapist.

Alternate Therapies

As the name suggests, alternate therapies are the therapies that provide an 'alternative' to convention medicine. The key characteristics of these therapies is that they are not tested like the conventional ones and hence never gets approval from the medicine community or national approval agencies such as FDA in the US[25] and EMA and MHRA in the UK[26] . Generally, the traditional remedies such as Ayurveda, homeopathy or Unani are the key treatments that have roots in our traditions, the traditions of bygone eras and of simpler world. These treatments make use of nature to cure anything that has gone wrong *in* nature i.e., inside our bodies. However, since these remedies are ancient when the world was much simpler – when there were no toxins or radiations, no pollution and no environmental loss. In those simpler times of 'organic'

[25]FDA – Food and Drug Administration (Government agency)

[26]EMA – European Medicines Agency; MHRA- Medicines and Healthcare products Regulatory Agency.

living, cancer as we know today did not exist and any abnormalities were treated in much earlier stages by using the herbs and minerals in all known medicinal systems. But the cancer as we know now is a modern phenomenon and is primarily a modern disease and a direct result of our modern industrial lives filled with pollution, toxicity, poor diet and stressful living. Since these factors continue to rise exponentially across the globe, that's why we see the alarming rate at which the cancer cases are rising as well.

It's not that these 'alternate' medicines are not being used these days. They are *definitely being used* but under the wider umbrella of nutrition (discusses ahead), effectively not as an alternate medicine but a complementary one. If one searches on Wikipedia for text "List of unproven and disproven cancer treatments", one can see a big result set of all the ineffective and unapproved alternate treatments for cancer.

Still, I researched on the Internet for any modern 'alternative' treatments that I could consider. Of all the treatments, I made some detailed research on the following ones. Primarily, I was looking for the testimonials from the patients, and for GBM if possible, as a benchmark for the success of these therapies. Here are some of the options:

Rigvir: The only reason that I have put this therapy on top of the list is because this was the only treatment I had considered to undergo, should my conventional treatment at MVCC ever fails me and should I ever get desperate to save my life. The Latvia based 'Global Virotherapy Cancer Clinic' had published some successful stories and testimonials of 'oncolytic'[27] treatment of certain cancers such as Melanoma (skin cancer). When I checked their website for testimonials on Melanoma, I found that Rigvir is registered in Latvia as officially approved treatment for melanoma, but I did not find any testimonial on GBM as such. When I contacted the clinic, they were frank that they have yet to conduct trial runs on GBM. That's when I decided to put this treatment in my wish list and as a last resort, should it ever come to that.

Gerson Therapy: Provided primarily by Gerson Institute in California, USA, their website (www.gerson.org) claims

---

[27]Virus natural or synthetic that kills the cancer cells only and not the normal/healthy cells.

250

– "The Gerson Therapy is a natural treatment that activates the body's extraordinary ability to heal itself through an organic, vegetarian diet, raw juices, coffee enemas and natural supplements". Curing just by organic food sounded too good to be true. When I searched their website carefully, I could not find statement that the treatment could cure my brain cancer i.e., GBM. Moreover, since it was all centric around juicing all day along, I wasn't very convinced with the approach towards the treatment of cancer in general and GBM in particular. Eventually, this therapy too fell from my radar, but the key point that I noted from this study was that 'nutrition' is *the key* that can be used alongside the main treatment, that I was receiving from MVCC.

Hyperthermia: The idea central to this therapy is that either whole body or locally effected areas are exposed to high temperature, between 40°C - 43°C with an intention to destroy the cancer cells. The 'local' hyperthermia claims are made on the basis that the cancer cells can be destroyed within a specific range and hardly anything alters with the surrounding normal cells. In order to raise the body temperature, the patient is put on a 'warming bed'.

251

Moreover, the further claim is that using the electromagnetic radiations, the temperature could be raised only in the designated area of tumor location and leaving rest of the body at its normal/room temperature.

I was skeptical of the claims because people living in earth's tropical zone are always exposed to these kinds of temperatures, and yet cancers are on rise in this zone as well. I wasn't convinced with these claims and further I could not find any statistics or 'credible' testimonials to this treatment, just a couple being attribute to the 'miracle' remission rather than a planned treatment. I had no option but to discard the 'miraculous' option as well. But, having said that, that is purely my view. I do not wish to discourage any patient from trying it out.

Nutrition

When I researched on nutrition in general and Gerson Therapy in particular, I was convinced that 'right' nutrition is the cornerstone of healthy recovery for every illness and Brain Cancer is certainly no exception. If a patient or a caregiver does not care for right nutrition, then no treatment provided by the medical science is going to be effective. That also implies that not only the oncologists, but patient too holds responsibility to cure himself or herself. This is because nutrition plays· most critical role to help body build its own immune system to destroy the cancer cells in the body and also to bear the onslaught of the toxic medicines that are given during the treatment.

The strategy behind nutrition planning is always to beat the cancer cells in their own move. In other words, if they starve the cancer cells of their essential feed, then we can plan nutrition so that whatever we eat, we do so to 'serve' the healthy cells and 'starve' the cancer cells; and for that, the differentiation between the nutrition is essential - the foods we *do* need to consume (cancer fighting foods) versus the food that we *do not* want to consume at all (carcinogen foods).

What kind of Nutrition

The fundamental principle behind the right nutrition during cancer (and otherwise) is to boost up the immune system of the body, so that body is capable of defending itself by destroying foreign harmful elements and of course including the cancer cells. This is because with right nutrition the body is perfectly capable to doing that. For a healthy individual, it helps to keep the disease like cancer at bay and for the victims, it still helps vastly to cleanse the internal system and boost up the immune system, thus giving essential support required to negate the toxicity that arise due to chemotherapy.

When it comes to application of the principle, the plan differs from individual to individual. The rule of thumb is that during illness such as cancer, and when the patient is undergoing any treatment such as chemotherapy, a patient must eat whatever suits to the patient, but as long as it is nutritious.

However, there are some general principles that the patient and the caregiver must be conversant with.

Cancer cells primarily *thrive on sugars* and clearly eliminating sugars from our diet is absolutely essential and first step towards healing. Hence, the only pragmatist option is to find ways to deny sugars to the cancer cells by denying sugars to the body itself. For some patients, who had loved sweet and sugary foods all their lives, it is not an easy task, but they still have to swallow a bitter pill by sacrificing any form of sugars from their diets.

Cancer cells also multiply in *absence of oxygen*, contrary to normal cells for which the supply of oxygen is absolutely vital. It is clearly not possible to deny oxygen to the body; so, a cancer patient must intake fresh oxygen as much as possible. If the patient is mobile than patient must aim to walk in the fresh air as much as possible, otherwise sitting in fresh air should also be beneficial.

Another strange thing that goes wrong during cancer is an *excess* growth of unstable 'free radical' chemicals'[28] in the body. These chemicals; generated externally or internally; are unstable and look to 'pair up' all the time to become stable. Usually, this is a normal functioning of our bodies and there is nothing unusual in this process. Ideally, they find their pair in other set of chemicals, which we get from our diet, called 'anti oxidants', thus giving stability to free radicals and of course to the whole body, eventually

---

[28]For detailed information, see http://www.healthchecksystems.com/antioxid.htm

building our immune system. However, when the growth of free radicals is in excess, caused by external factors such as by pollution or smoking, then the body finds it more difficult to generate the 'anti oxidants' from the normal nutrition and free radicals keep growing, ultimately creating threat to the body in form of diseases such as cancers.

Last but not least is the problem of *mucus*. The cancer cells not only thrive on sugars but also from the mucus especially that originate in gastrointestinal tract. Milk and milk products are the main culprits that generate the mucus. That implies that the dairy milk also must be cut off from the main diet of the patient and must be replaced with the unsweetened milks such as from hemp, almonds or from soya.

The problems of sugars, free radicals and dairy products could be sorted to an extent by planning nutrition specifically aiming at denying these agents. This happens when the patient consumes diet that is very rich in antioxidants and several essential minerals and vitamins for example, Vitamin E and Vitamin C. These vitamins aka the antioxidants stabilise the free radicals and yet manage to retain their own stability. Though the patient gets tempted to get the 'supplements' of these vitamins on top of the normal diet, but often these dosages have potential to destabilise the 'balanced diet'. The best solution is to eat Vegan food i.e., no meats and no foods derived from animals such as milk or yogurt to cheese. The Vegan intake must be 'organic' as much as possible. When in doubt, the patient must consult the physician or the nutritionist.

Sometimes the mineral and vitamin deficiencies must be corrected as well to boost the immune system of the body, which could be regional at times. For example, in the cold countries, in temperate zones, there is always very little sunshine compare to the tropical zone, resulting in deficiency of essential Vitamin D in all the inhabitants. In such case, the physicians have no problem in prescribing Vitamin D to patients. Similarly, if the weather is prone to giving cold and viral fevers, the patient is prescribed with Vitamin C supplements as well.

For general planning of the diet, the patient has to go back in the childhood to search for his/her favourite foods and as long as they are healthy, the patient would prefer that. For example, in my childhood days, I was not a very 'milkish' or 'creamish' person and milk and its products were the last things that I ever wanted to eat. In fact, I was allergic to milk. Also, I have never been a 'sugar' craving person. In fact, I never ate a bar of chocolate ever during my childhood and teenage. I have always been a 'spice' and 'root ingredient' lover. What I did use to love was the parathas stuffed with Potato, Cauliflower or Moolie (reddish). If not stuffed with these ingredients then I would love to have the root ingredients rich meals i.e., with lots of garlic, ginger, green chillies and onions. There was nothing unusual in this diet. I just happened to grow in semi-rural area in Punjab in India, where root ingredient-based diet just is happened to be the staple diet of the whole region.

This turned out to be blessing in disguise for me when I discovered that the cancer cells primarily thrive on sugars and mucus generated by milk products. That meant, I would enjoy the meals that had 'signature' on my DNA.

I happened to like the right nutritious food in my childhood, but that's not the point I am trying to make here. Instead, what I want to stress is that we all are same and if we inspect our childhoods, we will find natural, organic and clean food that we used to consume and love. Some people like me could have been consuming the root vegetables and some could have been consuming cruciferous vegetables. The stuff that we wish to eat during our illness must also be nutritious. Especially in case of cancer, it must suit the patient, particularly in the troublesome days such as during the chemotherapy.

Superfoods

There is no definition of super foods per se, but it is generally understood as nutrient rich food i.e., vegetables, fruits and nuts. The key to 'superfoods'-based diet is that it must contain lots of antioxidants to fight the free radicals and must contain minerals and vitamins to keep the body strong; and superfoods are a very good supply of vitamins and minerals essential for 'happy' and 'healthy' living. This is exactly what is being done under Gerson Therapy mentioned earlier.

Even though the Internet is filled with information on nutrition and healthy diets and there are thousands of books and magazines on the same subject, but below is the summary of my own research during my treatment days.

Root Vegetable: As the name suggests these vegetables are essentially the roots of the plants that we consume. Since they are the roots, they manage to collect lots of important nutrients and antioxidants directly from the soil. Examples are ginger, garlic, onion, turmeric, carrots, turnips, parsnips and many more. When it comes to healing nothing beat these root vegetables in their tendency of releasing anti-inflammation agents in the body. If a person is not very fond of these root vegetables, then their taste can always be disguised under something else, that is less controversial. For example, carrots or its juice is enormously good for any cancer patient. In this case the other ingredients such as ginger, turmeric or a dash of spirulina (discussed ahead) could easily be added. This could turn out to be the most beneficial antioxidant diet for the patient.

Berries: Superfoods from the berries family are not only rich in essential minerals and vitamins, but more than that, they contain highly potent antioxidants. For example, acai berries, blue berries, goji berries, raspberries, strawberries, blueberries, mulberries, bilberries, goldenberries and of course cherries. If for some reason a patient doesn't feel like consuming fresh berries, then alternative could be to make a smoothie of these vital superfoods and consume as much the body demands. Herbal infusions or teas made from these vital berries are sold as well. But ideally, a patient must aim to consume whole fresh berries or their smoothies instead of any derivatives, as the teas have very little dose of the key ingredients. Of course, as a last resort, for example when patient's chemotherapy is at peak, the frail body can consume tea.

Cruciferous Vegetables: From the cabbage family, it has been found that the phytochemicals found in cruciferous vegetables can stimulate enzymes in the body that detoxify carcinogens before they damage healthy cells. Another way cruciferous vegetable may help to protect against cancer is by reducing oxidative stress, which implies the overload of harmful molecules called 'oxygen-free radicals', which are generated by the body.

The following are the examples of cruciferous vegetables: Arugula (also called rocket salad), Broccoli, Kale, Mustard Greens, Collard Greens, Cabbage, Cauliflower, Brussel Sprouts, Bok-Choy and Watercress. No nutritionist would deny their importance in healing the body, but still the physician and/or the nutritionist must be consulted at all times while consuming these vegetables to make sure they do not interfere with the medicine protocol that the physicians are trying to administer on the patient. Needless to remind, these vegetables must be properly washed in clean water before consuming them and patient must strive to source them organically grown.

Spirulina Algae: Don't feel disgusted if it is algae. Rather, it is extremely potent nutrient provider with unmatched benefits of concentrated proteins and antioxidants, required for body's immunity. The 'organic' spirulina implies it has been grown in non-contaminated ponds and water bodies. That makes it very pricy superfood; in fact, the costliest one in the world per gram. Its cost can be easily up to 30 times more than the organic meat protein per gram. But its benefits easily outweigh its price; especially when just a dash if this algae is required given its extremely highly concentrated protein and antioxidant contents. As mentioned earlier, for example if added to carrot juice, spirulina works in synergy with antioxidant rich carrot juice.

Graviola: Last but not least, are the supplementary tables or syrup made from a fruit called Graviola, also known as Soursop. It is highly potent fruit and a highly recommended as alternate therapy to any kind of Cancer, Clearly, since none of the natural foods undergo scientific scrutiny, its potency has never been clinically tested, but since it is found in nature and fruits is certainly edible, there is absolutely no harm in consuming it.

A native of South American continent, especially in Argentina and Brazil, it made its way to India as well and where it got a name 'Laxman Phal' and is sold in plenty as fresh fruit and as many of its derivative such as juice, powder, tablets and capsules. The good thing is it can be consumed in either of the form. I have been consuming 4 tablets of 2000mg since the start of my treatment and never bothered to search for fresh fruit in the UK.

How to consume

There are lots of other super foods such as wheatgrass and turmeric, where the patient has to consume relatively large quantity of the food to get real benefit. In such cases it is advisable to buy the 'supplements'; of course, with the permission of the patient's oncologist or the nutritionist. For example, turmeric has clearly lots of antioxidant and anti-inflammatory properties, and in order to the intake effective, the patient has to consume large portions of it, which is not practical on day-to-day basis. In reality however, it is just a special extract called 'curcumin' within turmeric that does the magic. Whole turmeric being out of question, the patient may opt to take naturally produced curcumin supplements instead.

Such is the case with other essential ingredients such as Vitamin C, Vitamin D and Zinc tablets. Needless to remind, these supplements must be taken after due approval from the oncologist/physician/nutritionist.

Supplements – Last Note

Supplements are used to fill in the gaps left by the nutrition, effectively making up the ideal 'balanced diet'. During illness, these could become essential due to grave impact on body by the cancer drugs. But almost all the nutritionists and physiologists will recommend taking a healthy and well-balanced nutrition without relying on the supplements. In actual however, it is not possible to have all the essential nutrients from the diet alone and hence the need for supplements. However, under no circumstance should a patient (or even a healthy person) attempt to take supplements in excess of the prescription (by the nutritionist or as mentioned on the label of the supplement) as they are perfectly capable of overdosing the body with nutrients if they are already part of the healthy diet, and eventually building toxicity in the body. I state that because I have actually experienced this episode during my chemotherapy when the supplements had induced liver toxicity that was revealed during my blood test.

Again, to stay sure that right supplement is being used, the patient must consult his/her oncologist, who in turn will rely on the blood tests to prescribe the supplements and right dosage of them.

Emergency measures

Often a patient takes a hit during the treatment and the immunity of the body drops radically. This generally happens when a patient comes in spade of flu or viral during the chemotherapy therapy. In fact, it did happen to me during the last couple of cycles of the chemotherapy and as narrated in Part 1 of this book earlier. My platelet count had dropped to worrying levels and had to be boosted up, which called for an emergency measure.

In order to bring the platelet counts to the right level, I and Anu had come up with a remedy – a remedy of spinach soup, with a good quantity of ginger and garlic and a dash of organic spirulina powder. Just using this remedy had restored by platelet levels to the acceptable levels.

The key message here is that Spinach is an extremely good source of Iron and best way to fix iron deficiency as an emergency measure and for a healthy person, a habit of spinach soup 3-4 times as week should not do any harm at all. While spinach builds up the iron levels, ginger, garlic and spirulina provide the anti-inflammation agent. Together these vital ingredients work in synergy and effectively reboot the whole body.

Daily Diet Plan

I have made a diet plan that I aim to follow religiously. This is shared in the table below:

Around 6:30 AM Bed Tea with Soaked Walnuts (approx. 12 halves) and Almonds (approx. 8), brazil nuts (approx. 4) along with organic dates (2-3).
Around 9:00 – 9:30 AM Breakfast - 2 organic eggs omelette with wholesome organic root ingredients (garlic , ginger, green chillies, fresh coriander and of course onion) served with organic health bread made of hemp seeds, rye seeds, sunflower seeds, pumpkin seeds etc. These breads are much healthier than the normal wholemeal breads. Two tablets of Graviola (2000mg) immediately after that along with the prescribed medication of Levetiracetam (500mg), a stroke preventive steroid.

Around 11:30 AM
Brunch - Smoothie of Kale/Spinach leaves with berries (strawberry, raspberry, blueberry etc) and handful of red/black seedless grapes with half teaspoon of Spirulina.

Around 1:00 – 1:30 PM
Lunch - Homemade organic vegetable(s) with two stuffed chapatis of grinded mix of various seeds such as chia seeds, sunflower seeds, pumpkin seeds etc. Lunch to be followed by organic supplement tablets of Curcumin (2,500 mg), Vitamin C(2,500 mg), Zinc (80mg), Vitamin D (4000IU/100 microgram) and Cod Liver Oil(1,000 mg)

Around 4:00 – 4:30 PM
Evening snack 1 – Tea of Goji Berries along with a couple of dried figs.

Around 7:00 – 7:30 PM
Evening snack 2- Fresh fruits such as Papaya, Apple, Orange(s) and one "spotted" banana, sometimes as a smoothie or some healthy soup of carrots or mixed lentils.

Around 8:30 – 9:00 PM
Dinner - Usual homemade dinner just as in lunch (sometimes organic chicken or white/pink fish) along with fresh green salad. 2 chapatis are stuffed again with the grinded mix of various seeds.

Daily Routine (along with Diet Plan)

- Relax and enjoy the day with my family (when around) – even though my wife is at work all days and kids at school. And 40 -60 mins nap around 2:00 PM.
- Write Software for my own websites – this gives me immense joy and satisfaction.
- Occasionally, do gardening and look after kids' needs.
- Occasionally, listen to relaxing and calming music such a very gentle Santoor (Pt. Shiv Kumar Sharma) or gentle Tabla (Ustad Zakir Hussain)
- Light exercise at my home gym in evenings (6 days a week for 40-45 mins between 5:00 PM – 6:30 PM).

- Sound sleep (the above activities automatically result into this)

Resources:

1. https://draxe.com/what-are-superfoods

Attitude

Attitude is a little thing that makes a big difference.

- *Winston Churchill*

Weakness of attitude becomes weakness of character.

- *Albert Einstein*

Every person holds a set of two attitudes- one from two of the possible mental states and another one is spiritual. The mental attitude, that originates from the thought processes, could be *positive attitude* or *negative attitude* and the *spiritual attitude* on the other hand is, well - spiritual.

At a given point, positive and negative attitudes cannot co-exist and only one will reign along with its conjoined twin, spiritual attitude. The dominating mental attitude of the person, positive or negative defines the person and determines her/his character. The spiritual attitude on the other hand is the product of the mental attitude that the person holds and reinforces the same attitude [mental] further.

Let's discuss these three attitudes further.

Negative Attitude

There is a valid reason that I have mentioned negative attitude ahead of positive attitude. And the reason for that is, the negative attitude is far more prevalent in the world compared to the positive attitude and I do not need to give any proof of this statement because I am sure you see it around all the time, no matter which part of the world you live in. But suffice to say that over 98% of people possess negative attitude and it is barely 2% of humanity that has 'managed to acquire' positive attitude.

If this split of 98% vs mere 2% has shocked you, then turn on the world news and categorise the news into negative and positive groupings yourself. Alternatively, look around yourself an observe the people around you and then categorise their thoughts or traits as per the table 1 below.

Negative Traits	Positive Traits
Selfish	Considerate
Jealous	Understanding and tolerant
Catty or Spiteful	Pleasant and Kind
Manipulative (in nature)	Clear, frank and honest (in opinions)
Cheat and dishonest	Honest and Integral
Suspicious	Trusting and self-confident
Superstitious	Rational and Intellectual
Shallow emotions	Emotionally Intelligent
Oppressor	Benevolent
Non- committed (towards a cause or purpose) i.e., a Drifter	Fully committed and dedicated. i.e., a non-drifter.
Tendency to fail or possess thoughts of failure	Upbeat and believe in winning

Table 1: Comparison of Negative Attitude vs Positive Attitude.

If a person you spot seems to possess even a single negative trait, he/she will get categorised on the left side of the table and the reason being, just a single negative trait is enough for a person to acquire overall negative attitude, and further, the person with a negative attitude will still accidentally expose at least one of the negative traits even if he/she manages to suppress all others.

Comparatively, a person with positive attitude will also demonstrate only one of the positive traits at a time. Either that person will display other attitudes later or shall acquire relatively soon. One positive trait attracts another one.

Observe yourself how many people do you meet every day that have negative traits and how many people do you meet with positive traits. Your observation might not be as exactly as my claim, but I am confident that your figure won't be too off from mine.

The reason negative attitude takes a dominance is because, it is the core of our nature and comes 'naturally' to us. Just like weeds that grow in unattended gardens, eventually taking deep roots in the ground. In the same manner the negative attitude is also very deeply embedded in our psyche; and often we are not even aware of its presence in us, and the negative traits that it leads to.

Though a lot more traits can be added to the comparison table above, but irrespective of how many traits we list - at the core of every negativity, there is just one underlying emotion or instinct that give rise to *negative attitude* and that is the emotion of *Fear*.

Fear

As per the dictionary of Cambridge, the definition of fear is – "an unpleasant emotion or thought that you have when you are frightened or worried by something dangerous, painful, or bad that is happening or might happen".

The Six Basic Fears identified by Napoleon Hill in almost all his books are – fear of poverty, fear of criticism, fear of ill health, fear of loss of love, fear of old age and the strongest of all – the fear of death.

Clearly, fear is something negative that is capable of bringing unwanted or unpleasant reaction in one's body or mind, often to both. The mental reaction generally triggers the physical reaction and these physio-psychological unpleasant reactions often comes with change of behaviour such as tendency to cower or hide or tremble whenever there is any danger or trouble. This is called *flight* response by the subject to run away from a real or perceived threat and wishing for the threatening situation to be over. Sociologists and Psychologists also tell us that the fear could also result in an opposite reaction to *flight*, called *fight*. Hence the name of the famous psychological syndrome of *'fight-or-flight response'*, coined by American physiologist, Walter Bradford Cannon in early 1900s.

In the *fight* mode of this syndrome, the subject's mental reactions give result to anxiety in a situation of danger or trouble. Instead of cowering, subject's natural reaction is of fightback; instead of tendency to hide, the reaction of the subject is to 'counterattack' the aggressor. This *fight-or-flight* behaviour is not specific to humans and often can be seen amongst animals including our pet animals such as dogs and cats.

Both the fight response and flight response are natural and are triggered by subject's nervous system aka the brain, that further depends what sort of psychological training that brain / mind has received.

In summary, no matter how the subject responds, but the underlying reason of the reaction is the same - *fear*.

For humans, it is not an end of the world. Every person who carries any form of fear, *can* learn to manage to control this fear-based fight-or-flight response(s), but the subject has to train himself/herself by taking lessons from a qualified psychologist or by doing in-depth research through books and/or journals. To control and stabilize my reactions when I was in 20's and early 30's, I had read a fantastic book called "Emotional Intelligence" by Daniel Goleman. The book is no doubt brilliant, but it is an uphill task to apply the tips in real life and the only reason is that the natural programming of our brain is enormously complex and to re-programme it to bring mental stability in self is not that easy. Moreover, one reading is never enough, the subject has to read and re-read it several times. However, if the subject perseveres, the effort is definitely worth it in the end because the beneficial results are obvious to the subject!

Origin and Cause of Fear

We are 'naturally' lot more driven by *fears* rather than *incentives* or *faith*, which is completely the opposite force of fears (more on this later). And the reason of that could be found if we look at the way evolution of mankind that took place for millions of years. This evolution for the Homo Sapiens was certainly was not a walk in the park. We evolved in jungles amidst all sort of threats around us. The natural selection demanded homo sapiens to pass the toughest possible tests in order to survive and thrive. For most of the time, homo sapiens evolved in jungles fighting the beasts and the wild animals and not to mention the further onslaughts of natural calamities such as heavy rains, floods and diseases etc. All these factors had induced uncertainly of *life* in us humans and *fears* got very deeply rooted in us. What that further implies is that the fears inside us are also millions of years old and they have very deep imprint in our DNAs.

That imprint of fear in our DNAs continued and was very much prevalent in our ancestors when they started to live in clusters of dwellings. In fact, if we study carefully the beginnings of the early civilisations, it can be observed that the humans had formed the cities for 'self-defence' and had come together because they had genuine *fear* of living scattered lives in tribes and helmets.

During the overall timeline of human evolutions, that runs into millions of years, the 5,000 or 6,000 old, the so called 'first' civilisations seem relatively very modern compared to that. If we have to scale it, and if compress the timeline of one million years into 24 hours, then the so called 'ancient' civilisations that were founded 6,000 years ago (for example the oldest known, Mesopotamian Civilization), would actually be just around 8 and half minutes ago. Our civilisations are that new! – and for rest of the time, fears were making headway deep inside our emotions and psyche, and they still do.

Recorded History of Fear

Unfortunately, the civilisations were not too much of respite for humans either as they were constantly engaged in conflicts. The jungle rules prevailed, and they were at wars all the time, killing the co-humans en masse. Again, all due to fear. The motto of these early civilisations was the same – "let us invade them, before they invade us!".

Amidst all this chaos, the early religions were invented.

Ancient World of Religions

I agree with philosopher Bertrand Russell that 'religions are based on fear'[29]. The argument makes sense to me to large extant because in the ancient times, as mentioned above, when the civilisation started to form across the world, it was fear that was a dominating force. The main fear that was inculcated into human psyche was the *fear of death* because nobody knew what happens to a person after that. With time, the fear started to take anthropomorphic forms such as devils, ghosts, demons, witches and other

---

[29]In his famous lecture and book – "Why I am not a Christian"

agents of *death* and *torment*. Since these negative imaginations represented 'cruelty' and 'death', they managed to make mark in the humans as well and ultimately humans too began to be cruel and devilish, though for name sake, they were becoming 'civilised'. That also gave opportunity to the manipulators of the societies to form religions that began to scare normal working people with the life after death in hell and tortures in hell. These fear-based threats were not restricted to only one religion, but it was consistent feature in all the ancient religions that flourished in every corner of the earth.

As the threats of these fear-based visualisations grew, humans began to counteract these fears by purposefully and artificially giving rise to *faith* that soon gave rise to positive representations of faith in the form of gods, angels, deities etc.

Eventually, gods were pitched against the devils, angels were set against the demons and heavens were camped against the hells. In spite of all that however, these 'dual headed' religions still could not pacify the humans because in spite of the good forces of nature, the evil and bad forces remained and that's why these forces were made central in every mythological tale. In all the ancient mythological tales, the forces of *goodness* exist only to combat and destroy the forces of *evil*, and goodness as such has no purpose, as if a 'standalone goodness' is meaningless and can only have meaning when pitched against or seen against evil. This split psyche soon had to give birth to the positive (progressive or creative) forces and negative (degrading or destructive) forces in earthly living of humans- and they did.

Medieval and Modern Eras

Fast forward to medieval eras. Ancient civilisations became ruins and medieval warlords began to prevail. The characters that flash to our minds are the like of Genghis Khan. Some time ago, incidentally, I had read on the internet, about him. He had decimated nearly 40 million people in the name of marking his 'Empire'. The huge number is inconceivable by any ordinary mind, but history contains ample proof of his brutalities. All his accounts can send chill down to anybody's spine. From psychological perspective, I observed that the underlying force of his draconian nature was nothing but a deeply rooted *fear of dying*. Later I discovered, after his father's death who was the chief of the tribe, the 9-year-old boy Genghis was expelled from his own tribe by his half-brother. Days later Genghis killed his half-brother, because his half-brother had proclaimed himself as the new chief of the tribe. For rest of his life, while serving as chief, he carried this *fear of death*, i.e., of 'getting killed' by his enemy and in this fear only, he kept culling humans mercilessly, wherever he went.

Yet, Genghis Khan is one example from the medieval history of humans, that is nothing but full of gory details, men's devilish nature and rampant killing of the innocents.

The key point here is that fear that was deeply rooted in human psyche, especially the men, since millions of years was still largely present in the middle ages and no wonder the history of the world of that time is full or bloodshed and greed for thrones, wealth, territories, religions and of course women.

The fear of death and misery continued in the modern history when the colonisation of distant lands started.

I personally mark the beginning of the 'modern era' of our 'recorded' history when Italian navigator and 'Colonizer', Christopher Columbus, first set his food on the Islands of Bahamas in year 1492AD. Beginning from there, the European countries soon started a race to acquire territories across the globe and had started to establish their respective kingdoms and then colonies. There was no land left where the people were not suppressed, and attempts were not made to colonize.

Along with the territorial expansion of the colonial powers came their religions and faiths, which often followed the tyranny. The minds already filled with fear were brutally exploited and were brought into the realms of new faiths and so called 'values' of the invaders. Their proud ancient civilisations were first spoiled and then decimated by the medieval era invaders and finally the victorious powers in the modern era wrote their 'distorted' histories, precisely speaking by the historians who accompanied the conquerors and the colonists. Without saying too much, the underlying instincts of the imperialists was nothing but fear; the same fear that had prevailed in the invaders of the medieval eras but was unleashed on the so-claimed 'listless' targets with epileptic zeal.

These fears continued to travel and still exist in our modern world. We have seen dictators such as Hitler, Mussolini and Stalin during the world wars who killed innocent civilians without any apparent remorse. Clearly, there is no doubt that these dictators were fear driven[30], and it were their fears only that gave them the madness to wage world wars and kill innocent people in hundreds of millions.

The same fear resides in the 'disillusioned' minds of the terrorists in the 21st century. Out of fear, they want to take the credits from their respective lords in the heavens. By killing people from other race or religion or colour, they think that the lord will entertain them in heaven and will save them from the devil and torments in his hell. How sad!

---

[30]It is obvious if one reads Mein Kampf or Rise and fall of the Third Reich, that Hitler was full of fear himself when he provoked the masses to back him. And Mussolini's case was no different either.

Summary: The key negative emotions[31] that are still prevalent in the world today are:

• Sadness (depression, despair, hopelessness, etc.)
• Anxiety (fear, worry, concern, nervousness, panic, etc.)
• Anger (irritation, frustration, annoyance, rage, etc.)
• Guilt
• Shame/Embarrassment

All these emotions originate from the negative attitude, that further has its roots in fear, and finally result into negative traits and acts. In the 21st century where we have made incredible advances not only in medical sciences and information technology, there is no reason why these negative emotions must continue to prevail. Using the vast tools of reasoning that are available to the humans, such as internet, people must empower themselves with reasoning and must get rid of millenniums old fears that still dwell in us.

---

[31]www.betterhealth.vic.gov.au/health/healthyliving/negative-emotions

Positive Attitude

Let me give you some relief from the sad writing on the negative attitude and *fear* above. I need it too! Finally, we can discuss something nice and sane - the positive attitude. The positive attitude stands starkly opposite to the negative attitude discussed above. It is everything that is based on *Faith* – the serene and strengthening faith.

The only force that can dispel *fears* is *faith*, but there is a big catch in that. Unlike, fear, faith does not come naturally to us, even though we can argue that along with possessing fears, humans have positive 'natural' emotions as well such as love, empathy and kindness. But the negative traits that give rise to fight-or-flight syndrome, outweigh the positive ones by far, hence the reason that misery still exist in the world in the 21st century.

The positive attitude, and hence faith, need training of the mind and the spirit and of the traits (as listed earlier in the Table 1 of this chapter) that our common sense tells are 'positive'. Moreover, positive attitude once acquired, has to be maintained all the time, which is easier to say then done, because that demands complete will power of the person. It is like applying continuous force to move water up 'against' gravity, opposite of the natural tendency of water to flow down 'with' gravity. In the same manner, efforts must be made to train the mind with positive attitude and moreover, these efforts must be sustained; because any slippage in sustenance of these efforts result in empty space in mind and spirit, that gets naturally filled with negative attitudes and fear, just like weeds overtake our garden if we do not maintain it all the time.

Faith

Faith is a deeply embedded force in us that makes us believe in the goodness or good outcome to the situation that is ahead of us, with results still unknown. In physiological speak, where exactly the faith originates from, it is not known, but what we do know is that it comes from somewhere deep in our soul, our spirit. It is in stark contrast to fear because it is something positive and gives us positive vibes and elating sensations. It is a voice that makes a direct connection with the mind of the person and tells "You can handle this situation" or "You can overcome this hurdle/challenge" or "You can win over the challenger" or in extreme situation of life and death- "You can survive". In contrary to the fear, that brings the unpleasant reaction in subject's body and mind, *faith* on the other hand brings serenity, strength and stability in the subject and maintains the sanity of the subject in any challenging situation. Instead of trembling, the person can withstand any storm by staying firm just like a firmly rooted tree with a strong trunk.

Conditioned with faith, the subject doesn't suffer from 'fight-or-flight' syndrome, but stays calm, firm and in control, in face of adversity. This happens when person has complete control over her/his emotions and the nervous system is trained in such a manner that it only generates the impulses of self-control, sanity and self-confidence instead of panic or anxiety. Such a subject is called 'Emotionally Intelligent" and often positive labels are attached to her/him such as 'brave', 'courageous', 'spirited' and many others.

Confidence

A key element that cannot possibly come close to the domain of fear is confidence. *Fear* kills confidence, but it is cherished by *Faith*. Where there is faith, there exists confidence as well.

Confidence is the belief system of a person that makes the person fully convinced in her/his values and decision and if the person is taking a stand on some cause or act, then the person 'knows' that her conviction is 100% justified and worth taking stand for. In other words, if a subject has a firm belief system, then the subject is capable of dealing with any adversity that challenges her belief system and the values it holds. If a person stands on one side of the argument with firmly convinced of her position, and even if the rest of world take an alternate and ill thought view, the person with belief will have courage to stand to its ground and its side of the argument, and rest of the world will sooner or later appreciate the person's value system.

As mentioned earlier, faith is good to acquire but unfortunately, it is easier said than done. The person has to continuously engage in activities that can strengthen the faith and completely expel fear from her psyche. Reiterating again, inculcating faith in a fear driven mind is an enormous task and could take well over a decade, may be more, to expel all traces of fear, conditionally the conscious mind is engaged all the time in identifying and dismissing all the fears that deeply reside in the psyche. The conscious thinking must be engaged all the time to acquire the weapon of reasoning and then with this empowerment gained from accurate thought, the conscious thinking manages to tame away all the fears. Should a person reach that stage, i.e., of uprooting all the fear from the psyche, the person feel relived from the fears, pats her/his own shoulders for making an effort and actually feels and realises faith getting deeply rooted in self. After that faith just becomes the core nature/character of the person. But a continuous maintenance of *faith* is must.

Trust, Faith and Belief

It is not surprising that words Trust, Faith and Belief are used interchangeably in our day-to-day communication; after all they are synonyms in almost all dictionaries of the English language. But I have always felt some difference in the 'essence' of these words, and I think this confusion must be brought into light.

Trust: The word 'trust' implies when we rely on something external to our own being, when wishing for some thing or some positive expectations from another entity, an event or some situation. For example, when a new government is elected, we place our 'trust' over it, that it will serve the nation better. Or we always 'trust' our old and best friends to stand with us through thick and thin. Trust often comes when our *mind* has done some *thinking* and have concluded that the so and so entity could be relied upon.

Faith: On the other hand, the word 'faith' is some positive vibe or instinct that resides deep inside our own soul or spirit. Faith cannot reside in anything external to the being; rather faith is something that can only resides 'inside' of that being i.e., us. Anything that resides outside of us, we 'put' our 'trust' to it but not our 'faith'. We can trust God or divinity that it will do good to us, but it is our own faith, which is inside us, that makes us put that trust on God or divinity, or anything else which is external to us.

Belief: The word 'belief' originates from something we call 'system of belief' and often used in the context of religion we follow. When we worship God, we worship with

'Belief' and in this context the other two words, 'Faith' and 'Trust' might not fit that accurately. The word 'belief' is also used in context of personal 'values' for example when we say – "I cannot do so and so act because it is against my personal 'belief system' aka the values I hold".

Origin and Cause of Faith

The origin of faith can be traced back to more or less to the same time when fear began to get deeply rooted in the humans. The desire to survive and instinct to live came into homo sapiens almost the same time when they were chasing away the beasts; after all, humans still exist is a proof of that. The humans passed the natural selection to have survived for millions of years. During this long journey, as their intelligence grew, the fear served as a stick for them and faith was the carrot. Similarly, humans survived through the natural calamities because of the same survival instincts that later developed into *Faith*.

Faith had always stayed with the humans throughout the evolution, the early civilisation of ancient time, the medieval eras and even till today. As long has humans exist on earth, faith will always be there. But unfortunately, as always fear would still exist and we can just hope that faith begin to take deep roots amongst us the humans and spread more and more so that eventually we flip around the fear-faith equation of '98% *fear*' versus '2% *faith*' to the other way around.

History of Faith

Even though the early civilisations are thing of the past, but no one can deny they did create the marvels that we revere even today. All the art and architectures of the monuments of ancient civilisations, Chinese, Egyptian, Mayan, Indian, Greek and last but not least Roman were the work of nothing else, but *faith*. The faith thrived in spite of all the challenges that the fears had posed in those times.

Ancient World of Religious Faith

Even though the faith was artificially invented in the religions, but the thinkers of the time had injected it with great reverence to the divinity and is so clearly obvious from the beauty of the written texts such as Bible, Torah, Vedas, Egyptian book of dead, Tao Te Ching, Upanishads,

Bhagavad Gita and last but not least Buddhists Sutras[32]. Another symbol of marvellous spirit of faith could be seen in seven 'ancient wonders of the world' and several Hindu and Buddhists monuments in Asia such as Great Wall of China, Ajanta and Ellora Caves of India, Angkor Wat of Cambodia and of course numerous Buddhist stupas such as Bodh Gaya in India.

Similarly, the imageries of Gods that were created were also meant to induce faith and strength in the 'worshippers', where they could use their belief in these Gods and trust them as the healers of their miseries and eradicators of their sufferings. The prophets and sages propagated the same force to the followers that if their system of belief is intact and they do the kind deeds and live lives as good human beings, then they can fully trust their lord.

Spiritual Attitude

---

[32]Other religious texts such as Guru Grant Sahib of Sikhism and Kitab-i-Aqdas of Bahai Faith are modern books, compiled in 1604AD and 1873 AD respectively. And the author considers that the Quran is a book of medieval era.

In one of the articles published on the website of University of Minnesota[33], I found a perfect explanation of spirituality, as follows:

"Spirituality is a broad concept with room for many perspectives. In general, it includes a sense of connection to something bigger than ourselves, and it typically involves a search for meaning in life".

The definition is so profound and beautifully abstract. It leaves the person to pick *something bigger than ourselves* and to *search for meaning in life*. Just these two clauses are enough to split the humanity because every person will interpret these clauses in her own manner. While determining these two aspects, depends what mental attitude does the person possess, positive or negative.

A person with a positive attitude will reason herself what this 'something bigger' could be and will generally do a primary research in establishing the identifying the biggest possible entity, which clearly is the infinite universe without boundaries, its infinite amount of matter scattered in infinitely large cosmic space and an eternal flux that

---

[33]https://www.takingcharge.csh.umn.edu/what-spirituality

flows through it, which of course passes through every matter in the universe and obviously through the person as well – as her soul or spirit. Once the person realises this passing of cosmic flux through her, then that person realises a magical integration with the cosmic, both in matter and in flux. The philosophical system of India called Vedanta[34] concluding the speculations of earlier sacred texts, Vedas, on these two forces, where matter is referred as 'Brahman' and the flux has been referred as 'Atma'. The same kind of analogy of matter and flux could be found in Aristotle's work of Metaphysics.

However, when we have negative mental attitude; unfortunately, we lack in mental strength to do any primary research; and instead follow the opinions of others. With several opinions and guiding masters, we fail to comprehend much and stop at the anthropomorphic forms of God(s) as highest possible entities. We fail to reason beyond that, staying completely un-appreciative of the infinite vastness around us and the real reason why humanity had to create these anthropomorphic forms to understand the divinity. Instead of comprehending the

---

[34]Literally means The End of Vedas.

vastness of the universe and the significance of its flux, we get engaged in shallow rituals that too performed by some middle person. This shallowness give rise to superstitions, where we become susceptible to hear and follow any absurd dogmas. The blind faiths weaken the person further, that results in the degradation of his/her values. When majority of the population falls into this category, the weak population eventually brings collective degradation of the society as well and the cycle of *fear* continues.

Drifters and Non-Drifters

Another aspect that sets apart the humans into positive attitude group vs negative attitude group is found in people's tendency to engage in 'definite' aim at a given time or to remain 'indefinite' and directionless all the time.

A person with a positive attitude aka faith, keeps clear aims to achieve and spend most of her/his energy in achieving those goals. Nothing else matters to the person. This type of person cannot be distracted from the purpose that she is following and is called as *Non-Drifter*. A non-drifter is

297

always engaged in her activity of 'soul' in accordance with 'virtue', that Aristotle called 'Eudemonia' in his classic book 'Ethics' and would not have time to let any kind of influence that could distract her from that path. A non-drifter mind is a strong mind that concentrates only on the objective to be achieved. Even if a non-drifter fails, s(he) gets up and start moving again towards the goal yet again. A non-drifter is blind and deaf to everything else, including any criticism of her work. The person is absolutely dedicated to pursuing her desires. Giving up is not an option for the non-drifters, they take lessons when they are down and apply what they learn at the earliest opportunity and thrive further. Their strong minds *reason* well and when they *research* anything, they do so firsthand and from authentic resources.

If anyone inquire the non-drifters of their aims and ambitions and should they choose to answer, then their answers are crisp and clear, what they are engaged in. Their decisions are based on the facts that have been carefully analysed and not based on the whims of self or manipulations of others.

The opposite of this type of personality and that carries a negative attitude, is without any goal or aim to follow. The person lacks any major purpose in life, neither have any concept of having it. Moreover, a person with negative attitude is generally too lazy to find any purpose worth living for. If the person spends any energy at all on any act, then this concentration is very short lived and the person gives up on the first instance of any resistance in pursuing the goals or will lose energy in trying to chase multiple objectives at the same time, without giving attention to any specific task at a particular time. The person will accept every opinion but won't be sure of anything. The person will start many tasks but will finish none. This type of weak mind is also susceptible to the influence, generally the negative ones.

In our modern world, for example, a weak mind could easily come under the influence the radical politicians or radical religious teachers or any other propagandas. The weak minds get influenced not by reasoning but with *manipulation* tactics by the leaders be it any field of activity. Terrorists are a clear example of our 21st century living. These people may seem to have animal instincts that they kill the innocent civilians, but we also know that these people are the ones who failed to think 'positively' for themselves, then got brainwashed by the mad manipulators such as radical preachers and finally, sent on to their 'missions' of killing the fellow humans.

Tendency to not to drift and stay focused on the goals is often acquired by a person during the childhood through parents or the immediate environment where child grows. Once that habit of non-drifting is formed, it stays with the person throughout her life. The converse is also true. The habit of drifting also has its roots mostly in the childhood, when the parents fail to stop exposing the child from negativities such a fear, superstitions, vanity etc. Often over protection and display of emotions by parents to the children can make them weak as well and the children fail to *think* for themselves; resulting in big morale crusher as the children grow.

When men and women grow up enough to choose their life partners, they bring their respective attitudes into the relationship. The combinational attitude then becomes the attitude of their relationship for rest of their lives. If the individual attitudes are positive for both the partners then the resulting attitude is not only positive, but that combinational attitude is a synergy of the both the attitudes. And this mind which is more than the sum total of two individual minds has been called a 'Mastermind' by some of the world's leading motivational authors such as Napoleon Hill.

However, even if one person brings the negative attitude in the relationship, then the combinational attitude results into extreme negativity and antipathy. The relationships become bitter and soon the partners part away leaving behind the remains of the toxic and broken relationship.

Hence, it becomes absolutely imperative that a person, man or woman, chooses a life partner with utmost care and must listen not only to the heart but also to the mind's values.

Tips to Induce Faith

It is not that a person cannot decimate the negative attitude and acquire positive attitude later in his/her life.

The person certainly can, but it takes effort to do the complete turnaround to make it possible. The person needs to take complete control of the negative mind, make a very deliberate effort to identify the negative thoughts, emotions and traits, possess a burning desire to get rid of them and then embark on re-training the mind for positive attitude. In fact, if a person can reason enough to identify the negative traits that reside in him/her, then more than half of the job is done, but unfortunately, most of the people do not have to kind of mental faculties or spiritual depth to figure the negativity in them and they spend most of the lives only carrying out their old habits and in drifting.

Once a person realises that a correction in his/her attitude is needed, then acquiring resources to flip towards the positive attitude is not very difficult, conditionally the person keeps persevering to acquire the positive attitude. It could be a long journey though, but a journey that is filled with extreme satisfaction and elation of spirit. I can share some tips that I had compiled for myself. If a person thinks that he/she is a drifter but would like to stop drifting and direct his/her life towards some definite goals, these here are some tips:

- First, don't rush to find your life partner and certainly don't 'jump' into relationship, thinking that love is 'blind'. Love is certainly not blind and must be lived with eyes and 'mind' wide open. We must be certain of the qualities and virtues we seek in our potential love and life partner. Any ill-thought trial with any person is not only risky but makes a person a 'drifter' for life. On the other hand, if one is sensible and look for qualities in a partner that supplements her own personality traits, that makes a 'mastermind' is a sign of full, long lasting and eternal love.

- Learn to do your own thinking and stop living on the advices of other people. This step may sound simple but is the most difficult of all. The key challenge is to condition the mind to identify all the fears that reside in person's psyche then to get rid of them one by one. For example, the fear of failure and fear of poverty, are not that easy to get rid of, and all these different kinds of fears that we hold inside us require different tactics to eliminate. Even if you fail when you apply your own mind and fail in attaining what you wanted, you won't have anyone else to blame, but yourself, and taking the blame on self is not going to destroy you but will correct you and energise you to keep moving.

- While a person undergoes in this self-correction of attitude and transition from fear to faith, it becomes imperative that the person continuously stays in the company of positive people and more important that that is positive 'thoughts', as mentioned in a brilliant book by Prentice Mulford named 'Thoughts are Things'. Not only that, there are several motivational books that could become person's best friend and could strengthen person's soul or spirit. I have listed my favourite books under 'Resources', at the end of this chapter. These books had become my best friends after my allegiance to them for 15 years.

- Similarly, to build a positive strengthening attitude, I have always felt that following examples of the personalities that had endured setbacks and emerged victorious in their cause and purpose is very important. A person may pick his/her own personal heroes, as it largely depends, what field the person is engaged in a most likely the person will pick inspiration from the legends from the same field. But the person needs to ensure that when seeking inspiration, the person studies the legends of the field, ideally who have changed the world for us. For example, if a person has aspiration in Physics then there cannot be better inspiration than Albert Einstein and on the other end if a person is in sports, there cannot be a greater legend than boxing greatest, Muhammad Ali. However, for person to acquire a positive attitude in general, heroes could be picked from any walk of life, be it sports, or cinema, or business or any other field. Extending the example above, there is no reason why a scientist in making cannot get an inspiration from the will power of Muhammad Ali and I don't see any reason why a sports person should shy away from reading Einstein to sharpen his/her intellect. Similarly, there are several 'moral' and 'spiritual' leaders such as Dalai Lama and Mahatma Gandhi. After all, to succeed in 21st century, an all-round mental awareness and spiritual strength is required.

- Keep the *horizon of the vision* clear, where you want to be and then follow your instincts to move towards that horizon. What paths you take and what interim goals you set are not that important as much as the knowledge and faith in yourself that you are on track towards that horizon; even if you might have to keep altering your path to reach to that horizon, for example should you ever face any adversity. An ideal scenario would be keeping a goal that would be impossible to attain within your lifetime. Elon Musk creates a perfect example for rest of the humanity today, when he dreams of taking humanity to the planet Mars within his lifetime and also when he says – "we must learn to do impossible on top of impossible". It is this vision of Musk that drives his ventures whether it is SpaceX or Tesla or SolarCity.

- Ensure that whatever you do, you can justify that you are rendering a useful service to humanity. Make sure that you believe in giving more to the world and take less in return. Again, the world is full of such examples .

- Should you wish for anything from divinity, then 'ask' for moral strength and courage to accomplish your goals, all by yourself and with your mastermind. But never 'beg' for anything material and never wait for any wonders or magic to happen.

- Expel any fear or doubt from you mind because fear is a devil that sits on your shoulder and continuously whispers to your mind all sort of things that keep you continuously in distraction, away from any goals or aims you might have. Instead, inculcate the habits that induce faith in your psyche. When you connect to divinity or infinite intelligence of the universe, feel at comfort with that force, because that faith will chase away the devil of fear.

- Realise that we play game with our Life. The non-drifters aka people with positive mental attitude live life at their own terms, but the drifters with negative mental attitude, let their lives dictates the terms of their insignificant survival.

Last Note: Last but not least, find love for science. It makes you think and dispels fear or 'blind' faith of anything you might hold. Legendary Steve Jobs once said – "Learn programming and you will learn the art of *thinking*". Of course, the word programming could be replaced with anything else, which is investigative or as long as it remains within the domain of science, where you need to use your mental faculties and logical reasoning. For example, one may wish to systematically investigate how a plant grows or how exactly our universe came into existence and where exactly it is heading to? The bottom line is there should be no irrational behaviour, no guess or speculative work involved in the thinking.

Resources:

Napoleon Hill : *Law of Success, Outwitting the Devil, Think and Grow Rich, Master Key to Riches and Success Through a Positive Mental Attitude (with W. Clement Stone).*
Robin Sharma – *The Monk who sold his Ferrari, The Saint the Surfer and The CEO and Life Lessons from the Monk Who Sold His Ferrari.*
Tony Robbins : *Awaken the Giant within and his YouTube channel 'Tony Robbins'*
Susan Jeffers: *Feel the fear and do it anyway.*

Epilogue

Be happy for this moment,
This moment is your life.

- Omer Khayyam

I am immensely grateful that I am still alive after almost six years since the diagnosis of GBM, the most vicious brain tumour known, giving just 15 months of median survival rate. During these six years, I had numerous scans each quarter of a year. All that implies is that I have survived the median by far. However, I still cannot say that I am fully recovered, and I certainly do not know what lies ahead and how much my life span would be from here. If I do any projections, that would be a false claim on my behalf, given the nature of the illness I had. From here onwards my survival strategy to be to stay calm, make an alliance with the cancer and shall try to eventually show it an exit from my body, very gently!

As per the latest scan I had on 28th April 2021 at MVCC, my oncologist, Dr Mulholland had pronounced my GBM tumour as a "controllable disease", since there were "no new or revived symptoms".

For me this status-quo of 'controllable disease' disease will do for now. I do not want to waste my time in speculating what could have caused it. Also, I do not know what state would come after this state and that is yet to be seen. So far, I am just keeping full faith in my oncology team and staying humble to accept whatever destiny has in store for me.

Yet, I am taking things as they come to me. Every day is a gift to me and a new life. I have already labelled it as my re-birth. I am trying to make Mahatma Gandhi's quote 'literally' as philosophy for my everyday living:

Live life as if you were to die tomorrow,

Learn as if you were to live forever.

Each day, I try to learn as much as I can on life as such and various other subjects that fills inside of me with calmness and serenity.

With Gandhi's quote as central philosophy of my life and at the same time, guided by Napoleon Hill's 'The Law of Success', I am trying my best to make a transition into my new life.

Definite Chief Aim

I had first bought Napoleon Hill's book 'The Law of Success' when, just after our marriage, Anu's father had highly recommended it to me. When I first scanned at the book, I got hooked. In each of four consecutive readings of this brilliant book, the chapter of 'Definite Chief Aim' was the main one to pop out. With each reading, some software idea would flash in my mind, I would start implementing and at first hurdle I would give up, just as Hill had warned in the book. By giving up that way, I had started to get frustrated and eventually shelved the book (even though Hill had warned in the same chapter that 98% people would just give up their aim on the first failure). I had started to feel guilty, when I shouldn't have.

But, now when I reflect on the frustration that I used to carry, I recall that the reason, I could never pursue up with any 'Definite Chief Aim' was because my young mind at time of 20's and 30s was cluttered with so many things that maturity of sorting the ideas in a priority list was never there – it was only an untrained and an untamed mind going wild that wanted to take a giant leap without waiting and did not have the patience to take small steps towards any arduous journey. I always knew the following quote from Thomas Edison but out of immaturity never fully grasped the depth and meaning of it.

The quote is:

"Good things come to those,
Who hustle while they wait."

Out of immaturity, I would envisage success as simply a matter of turning over a pancake on a pan. Clearly, when things did not work out, my failures filled me with frustration and anxiety and if that trend continues in any person, then eventually one gets nothing but a disease like I got.

I also had 'read' a lot of literature and biographies of the legendary figures, such as Mahatma Gandhi, Martin Luther King Jr, Muhammad Ali, Bruce Lee and others, but I never *studied* them *carefully*. They all had persevered before 'arriving'. But now, I have realized that failure is actually a part of journey towards success and if we fail, it only implies that we have lessons to learn; we must pick ourselves up and keep moving, without worrying how much time we have on this earth.

Now, with the suffering I had endured and when destiny has offered me with another chance, I want to play the game of life carefully, and live a life that must be filled with love and open heart for everyone; without of course being too hard on myself. During the recovery period of first two years, I managed to publish my memoirs (of course Edition 1 of this book) and had managed to launch my websites – www.gdfnow.org and www.bjmanch.in. For now, my aim is to publish this 2nd edition of the book and propagate my websites and then I shall move on to the other desires that I had always kept in the backburner as other things took more priority in the past, mainly to be with my children as much as I can and enjoy watching them growing.

Which exact path I am going to take after these ventures, I do not know yet. But the aim at broader level is clear: *to see this world a better, peaceful and beautiful place to live in, not only for me, my own children but for whole posterity.*

Lessons to Learn

As my life changes,
It gives me new things to write about.
-Jason Isbell

I need to learn to be calm and collected while taking these steps towards the goals I am going to set for myself, starting from the publishing of this edition of the book and propagating my websites. If you are reading this book then just assume that I have already moved towards my next goal that will serve the 'Definite Chief Aim' of my life i.e., *'to see this world a better, peaceful and beautiful place to live in, not only for me, my own children but for whole posterity'*. As long as I am alive, I shall not let any negative thought upset my mind and shall only embrace the positive thoughts that will help in reaching the next goal. I am greedy to an extent that I do want to survive and live till my next goal ends and don't care much how many goals I reach during the impossible journey to the horizon I see.

I have finally realized that rushing never helps. When in my previous life, I would assume a long life, I did nothing but procrastinate. Now in this second lease of life that I have got, I have realized that I had taken my life for granted. Now when it all looks uncertain to me, when I don't know what's in store for me tomorrow or in my next

MRI scan, I try to live everyday as much as I can and want to cherish every moment of my life.

For every moment I want Anu, Zoravar and Nimrat to be around me, keep giving me the positive vibes and love and keep motivating to reach my next goal. I still want to be ambitious and hardworking, but I do not wish to take any ill thought risks.

Only during my suffering, I learnt that patience could have been the key to get to my objectives. What my healthy and exuberant mind could not conceive back then, my cancer ridden mind is surprisingly reasoning now. In spite of that I do not carry any regrets, because I *know* that whatever I did, I did it for a reason; to become a self-made man.

I feel grateful too that I have survived and have learnt the lesson albeit the very hard way. But that's what Napoleon Hill also warned when he wrote "*The best education is the education you receive in the University of Hard-knocks*" and "*everything academic that we acquire in universities and colleges is just an encyclopaedic knowledge and have no relevance if we do not learn how to apply that*". It is so true. None of the academic things that I studies all my life, are helping me when I want to survive for decades. Instead, the survival thoughts originate from the training that I gave to my soul and my spirit.

Now my serene and calm mind (in spite of carrying cancer) could make a sense at last of such a noble and beautiful concept, that I had completely distorted in my previous life. I would say, this particular realization proved a turning point in my whole healing process. On the face of potential death, I have learnt what 'patience' actually means. I had never prayed to anything or anyone but this time I am truly wishing for a new spell of life, not for any material goals but for capacity and will to work creatively so that I could leave something behind that at least my children should feel proud of. Well - if I continue to survive, then all four of us would be a team and I will live my dreams to the fullest.

I have also realized that all the ideas that I tried earlier and then gave up on the first hurdle, had the same underlying theme of '*to see this world a better, peaceful and beautiful place to live in, not only for me, my own children but for whole posterity*'. I have learnt that as long as that vision is held with clarity, I shouldn't mind whether a specific idea succeeds or not.

If I had not decided to shun my old style of thinking that was filled with *fear* and if I had not declared to myself that I am embarking on a new lease of life with *faith*, I would have continued to be a negative thinker. I would have denied myself the power of such a simple philosophy and concept. But now, I am focused on not repeating the mistakes because in my new life, my first goal post is to finish this edition of the book as soon as possible along with propagating the websites, so that the book lands in the hands of the readers like yourself and the websites to change the world piecemeal.

If I keep *faith* and the view of my horizon clear, then I must not worry about the path I take, I can just start walking towards the horizon and the paths could keep changing. I realized that while walking, should I fall down, I must pick myself again and get on moving again because as Richard Branson says – "*falling forward on your face still implies you are going forward*". At no point I want to have time to waste. Every breath I take now is a precious gift to me from the divinity.

During my illness when life seemed uncertain, I had just started to wish for recovery, like I never did and started to beg for a new life; but to whom, I do not know. The Moment I wake up in the morning, I pray unashamedly to the cosmic to contribute towards my aim - '*to see this world a better, peaceful place ...*'.

When I underwent my first three scans from April'27th, I was keener to see whether I had been granted a new lease of life. When the subsequent scans started to come out to be 'all positive', I had a great sense of relief and immediately thoughts had started to become even more clearer. I realized that the journey to achieve whatever we want to achieve must bring 'Eudemonia' to us, which as per Aristotle in his book, The Ethics suggests – "*Eudemonia is more than happiness. It is an activity of soul in accordance with virtue*". If we are clear where our Eudemonia lies and as long as we know that we are working towards that, then the specific goal posts do not matter. If I fail on first attempt, then I must learn and aim to succeed in second one and still if there is a failure then I must not get upset and must keep trying over and over again. I just want to keep trying till I have succeeded in my own conviction, because I am not going to permit myself quitting at any point. I just have to keep moving till I am alive – without fear!

We must keep moving forward. That's it! We'll reach home sooner or later and that would be a most joyous moment. We just need to keep taking steps. As we keep taking these steps, we not only get closer to the horizon that we saw from the distance, but we keep learning as well - from books, other people's lives and from our own experiences of life and the journey. These learnings keep refining our vision in the sense that horizon stays the same but with learnings, we can keep changing our paths without much trouble and we can overcome the setbacks or 'temporary failures' with relative ease.

And last but not least, I have realised that we can't all be captains, there has got be a crew as well. And:

> *If you can't be a tree, be a bush,*
> *and if you can't be a bush, be a grass,*
> *but "be".*
> -   *Douglas Malloch*

Another aspect of life that I have learnt during my illness is that often we make life overly complex. We just need to focus on our destination and keep playing just like the game of snakes and ladders. Sometime, life will give us ladders to climb up quickly and sometimes we will encounter the snakes as well that will throw us back. Yet we must keep throwing the dice and keep enjoying the game – of 'life'!!

My Healers

> *Lots of people want to ride with you in the limo,*
> *But what you want is someone*
> *who will take bus with you when the limo breaks down.,*

- Oprah Winfrey.

Though I do not know specifically what the reason behind my recovery has been so far, but what I do know is that unconditional love and care during my most difficult days made me heal immensely.

Immediate Family

I received immense love, care, assurance and support from not only Anu but also from Zoravar and Nimrat at all times. They had turned into angels of my life who brought healing and relaxation to me at all times. I had always felt that I had fallen into the pit of darkness but when I looked at their faces, I saw light that would motivate me and reinforce my belief in love and life. I wanted to get better by 'tricking' the illness to defeat because I wanted to spend rest of my life with them and wanted to see Zoravar and Nimrat grow. There were times, when I used to be very pessimist and felt no strength to lift myself up, but their love would always inject fresh burst of energy into me. I would then lift myself up and move on.

I had always felt that it has not been fair on them, because my illness had stolen a portion of their childhood and compelled them to grow mature before their age. When it was time for them to grow up and my time to show them the beautiful world outside, they were trapped inside the house with me. Now that I feel better and back on my feet, I want to make an attempt to make up for their losses and aim to give them attention and affection as much as I can.

Anu too kept tremendous patience with me and gave me immense affection and love during my cure and recovery. I had always loved her from the moment I first set my eyes on her but her support in this most difficult period of my life made me immensely grateful and proud of her by my side. I always wonder, how many people in the world would have looked after another like she did and at the same time strengthening my spirits and will to live on.

Wider Families

Similarly, I received true affection from my parents' side as well. Just talking to everyone on the phone would give me the vibes of healing. I don't know if it is called 'sixth' sense or something else, but there was something that was travelling from them to me across half the globe.

Mother searched frantically for alternative 'natural' remedies for my cure and my father too did not leave any stone unturned to look for potential remedies that could cure me. Mother later told me that father had been getting up very early in mornings to say prayers for my full healing and recovery. I am sure their prayers and wishes have worked so far and shall continue to keep me alive.

My family of in-laws was also radiated the same warmth. They too wished a lot for me, and when in the UK, looked after me enormously. I always knew that the family is very kind and caring, but when I received personal attention from them, I had started to admire and respect them even more.

Support and love from my families did a double and triple coating of love on me over my immediate family and I must admit that I received three times more comfort and hence three times more healing.

In summary, I would say that in these critical moments of life, it is very essential to have loved ones around and their wishes and prayers do heal.

Neighbours and Friends

We happen to have very good neighbourhood, and everyone wished me well all the time. There are at least 10 families around us who would always say that they "keep sending their best wishes to my door all the time". And I would always tell them that their wishes had been indeed coming to me and had been working magic on me. Every time I stepped out of the door, if either of the neighbour meets me, s(he) would instantly inquire about my health and would always offer their help should I ever need any and would always convey to me the best of health and recovery.

I do have some good friends in the UK and other parts of the world, including of course in India, who would visit me at times and often call to inquire about my recovery. When I could talk, I would talk to them over the phone, else they would take briefing and convey wishes to Anu. Often, they would send their wishes on WhatsApp messaging. Another factor with friends is that apart from giving words of comfort, they would make me laugh over the phone calls and we all know that 'laughter' is one of the best possible remedy for all illness, if not the one.

NHS and Charities

Last but not least, NHS stood to its worldwide reputation of providing best possible treatments for the critical illness like of mine. Not only the treatment, but humanly touch that I received from NHS never made me feel that I am receiving a treatment that is short of any perfection. All the oncologists and nurses I met during the four years of the treatment, showed a true and genuine interest in my recovery.

Dr Paul Mulholland and head nurse Maggie Fitzgerald showed an extreme example of personal care and personal bonding with the patient. Meeting them itself had become a big healer for me and no matter what my condition had been, I always looked forward to meeting these kind souls so that I could heal my own soul.

I was recommended by Dr Mulholland to charities such as Lynda Jackson McMillan centre (within the premises of the MVCC hospital) and St Luke's Hospice (that was just a walking distance from my home). I exploited their services as much as I could, especially at St Luke's. I used the services of music therapy, physiotherapy and acupuncture therapy more than any other patient. It was partly my fault and partly theirs as they were being so considerate and kind. From Lynda Jackson, I received various services as well such as massage and aromatherapy.

My reading habits

I have always been fond of reading and even during the busiest times of my employments, I would be reading one book or the other, while travelling in London underground. The habit continued during my illness as well. Whereas previously I would read inspirational books but now as I lied on the bed recovering, I started to read more spiritual stuff as well such as translation of Guru Granth Sahib, Bhagavad Gita, Holy Bible, Eckhart Tolle, Frankl Viktor and others.

End Note: I am starting to realise the genuine desires of my soul. Eventually, I would like to '*take out all the stuff I have inside of my basement*'. In fact, I will have no regrets if I just manage to take my current ventures of publishing the book and take my websites to a respectable level. After that, I'll see where I stand but, in my horizon, a definite aim is clear and will finalise my next goal post after bringing these ventures where I want them to be.

Appendix A - GBM Primer

In this appendix, I have tried to compile very basic information on cancer in general and concluded the chapter with Brain Cancers including GBM.

Cell Basics

All humans are made of cells, the most basic building block of our body. There are trillions of cells in a human body, and they are all of different types, approximately around 200 different kinds. An example is shown below:

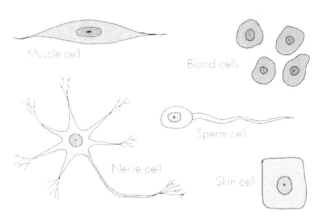

Fig A- Cell types in body. Source: http://haleo.co.uk/the-body/cells/

There are a couple of key characteristics of these cells:

First, they consume nutrition for the body and generate energy that is consumed by all body organs to perform their respective functions. Not to mention, they generate waste as well during this process, that gets expelled out by the body.

Second, with the exception of nerve cells, all other cells live for a limited time only and then they die their natural death to give way to newly formed 'daughter cells' by the process of cell division, which is a normal working pattern of a body. In fact, it is an essential biological process in all multicellular organisms. Nerve cells, on the other hand only grow till the body reaches adulthood and after that their count stagnates, and eventually start to die slowly with the age of the body; and finally, the leftovers dying only with the body itself. The nerve cells are also called neurons. Neurons are essentially the building blocks of the body's CNS (Central Nervous System), which of course includes the brain as well. More on the nerve cells/neurons later.

Blood Cells

Though all cell types are important for healthy functioning of body, but the most vital amongst the equals are the blood cells.

There are three different types of blood cells:

1. Red blood cells (RBC): They transport oxygen throughout the body and all its organs.

2. White blood cells (WBC): These are the defence cells in the blood that prevent the external harmful bodies from infecting the body.

3. Platelets: They help to clot the blood when there is any injury, cuts or bruises.

All these cells flow in a fluid called 'plasma' and all these four components together make the most special fluid of our body that we call blood.

This is shown in the figure below.

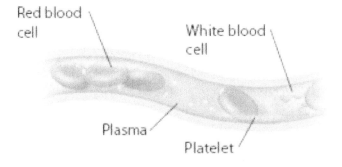

Fig B: Blood and its contents

Source: www.saintlukeshealthsystem.org

Another key fact to be noted is that RBCs are formed in red bone marrow of the body and these RBCs have short life span of around 100-120 days. After that they get automatically removed from the body and the daughter cells take over. The WBCs come next with even shorter lifespan of 13-20 days. Platelets have the shortest lifespan of all, of just 8-9 days.

What is Cancer

As mentioned earlier, in the normal functioning of a body it is very essential for cells to die at right time so that new cells could take the charge of the body. However, when the cells fail to replicate themselves, and fail to die their natural death, they continue to grow. The cause of this *irrational growth* is not known, but what *is* known that while new cells are being created, the old ones just refuse to die. If scientists could discover why the cells don't die, then the treatment for cancer won't be too far either. The cancer cells thrive on sugars, thus making sugar in any form, worst enemy of the cancer patient. Since sugar is highly acidic, with a pH of 6.4/10, it eventually turns the tumour highly acidic as well. The normal cells on the other hand stay alkaline at par with blood's normal alkaline levels of 7.4/10. If sugar is 'completely' withdrawn from the diet then not only the healthy cells start to starve, as the body needs a certain level of sugar to function properly, but also, the cancer cells began to consume other essential nutrients such as proteins and fats to generate glucose (sugar) that way. Essentially, these tumour or cancer cells start to act like 'gangsters'. They cut off the much-needed nutrition supplies to the new and healthy cells . Being out-of-control, they start to form lumps in body organ/s, and eventually start to disrupt the normal functioning of the body. Hence the word Cancer, which literally means *crab or creeping ulcer* in Latin.

The picture below shows how the Tumour or Cancer in formation.

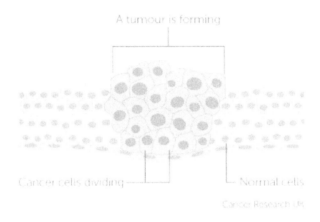

Fig C: The formation of Cancer.
Source: http://www.cancerresearchuk.org

Brain Tumour and Brain Cancer

Throughout the brain and spinal cord we all have neurons, which transmit electrical and chemical signals, or messages across the body. Surrounding the neurons are cells called 'glial' cells, as shown in Fig C here.

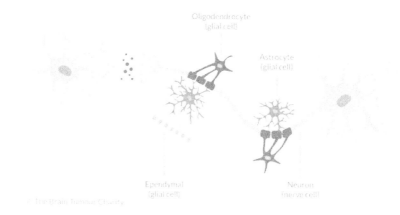

Fig D: Nerve Cell and Glial Cells
Image Source: The Brain Tumour Charity, UK

Unlike neurons however, the glial cells undergo cell division like all other cells. During their lifespan, these glial cells support and protect the neurons, provide the neurons with oxygen and nutrients, and remove the dead glial cells. Glial cells are much smaller than neurons and the brain has lot more glial cells than neurons.

All cancers are no doubt dangerous and not welcome in the body, but the most lethal of all cancers is Brain Cancer and there are reasons for that:

1. As mentioned above, the brain primarily is made of neurons and there is limit to which the neurons can grow. Once the

neurons are damaged or lost because of any defective glial cells or any other reason, then the neurons never grow again. However, since there are lot more neurons in the human brain, then they are ever used, in reality, if the neurons ever get damaged, then the neurons that had been lying dormant earlier are brought in the service by the brain automatically, taking the damaged ones out of service.

2. Brain is the most vital organ of the body. Because of its importance and complexity, it receives a special protection compared to other organs. First it resides in the skull, and second, within the skull, it is kept shielded from rest of the body by a membrane of tissues called as 'Blood Brain Barrier', or BBB for short. BBB acts like a seal and protects the brain from any foreign harmful substance that might make its way into the body.

3. The downside of BBB, however, is that it also prevents most of the cancer drugs reaching the brain, as these medicines are still perceived as a 'foreign substance' by the body. This is clearly is not a desired scenario for the patients with brain cancer.

4. The brain's only connection with rest of the body is via the spinal cord, making body's central nervous system (CNS). This connection of two most vital organs is very delicate and is protected with extreme caution by the physicians.

The Brain Tumour happens when there is an excessive growth of these glial cells on the same lines as any normal cell in any other part of the body and as discussed in the previous section.

With Brain Tumour, the first priority of the oncologist is to stop the tumour reaching the spinal cord and avoiding the spread of tumour in rest of the body hence avoiding what is commonly known as 'metastasis'. See Fig D below highlights the connectivity and sensitivity the Brain and Spinal cord joint.

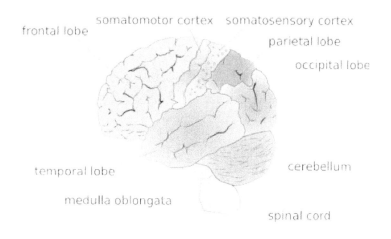

Fig E: Brain Diagram
Source: www.awesomestories.com/asset/view/Diagram-of-the-Brain

Brain Tumour, Seizure and Stroke

During its normal functioning, the brain also generates tiny electrical signals, that can be measured with Electro-encephalo-gram (EEG[35] as shown in Fig E ahead), thus making electrical activity as part of normal brain functioning. However, when a person carries a brain tumour, then the tumour can put pressure on the normal electrical activity, generating abnormal electrical activity in the brain that can result into 'Seizure' or 'fits'.

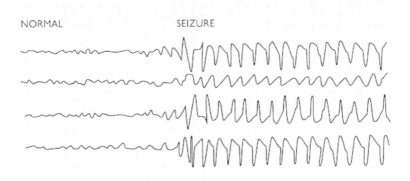

Fig F: EEG recording

Source: http://rrapid.leeds.ac.uk/ebook/06-dysfunction-04.html

On the other hand, a Brain tumour may start to apply pressure on the nearby healthy part of the brain and may block the blood circulation in the brain, triggering what we call as 'Brain Stroke' or simply Stroke.

---

[35] Just like ECG (Electro-cardio-gram) is used to measure heart activity.

Both Seizure and Strokes are the reason why oncologists prescribe steroids to normalise the electrical activity of brain and thereby preventing any potential seizure.

The downsize of taking these medications, however, is slow down in mental activity that eventually results into lethargy.

And, in order to prevent strokes, 'anti-platelet agents' such as aspirin, or 'anticoagulants' such as warfarin are generally prescribed. They act as 'blood thinners' and interfere with the blood's ability to clot and thus preventing strokes. As a side note, these blood thinners are also used to prevent heart attacks.

Grades of Brain Cancer

Brain tumours can develop from any of these types of glial cells. Glioma is the collective name for this group of tumours.

However, gliomas will also have a more specific name depending on which type of glial cell the tumour grows from.
Brain tumours that grow from astrocyte cells are called *Astrocytomas*.
Brain tumours that grow from oligodendrocytes are called *Oligodendrogliomas*.

Brain tumours that grow from ependymal cells are called *Ependymomas*.

Further, when Astrocytomas go unnoticed and when they become malignant, it is called *Glioblastoma* (GBM)

Brain tumours are graded by the World Health Organisation (WHO) in the range 1 to 4, according to how they behave i.e. how fast they grow and how likely they are to spread 'within the brain'. The following are the key classifications that WHO makes regarding the grades of the Brain Cancer:

Grade 1: Astrocytoma
Grade 2: Oligo Astrocytoma (a mixed glioma of Astrocytoma and Oligodendroglioma)
Grade 3: Oligodendroglioma
Grade 4: Glioblastoma (GBM)

Tumours graded 1 and 2 are relatively slow-growing, and are sometimes referred to as *low grade*, but they must be managed as soon as possible else they have tendency to develop.

Tumours graded 3 and 4 are *high-grade*, fast-growing, more aggressive tumours, sometimes referred to as 'malignant' or 'cancerous', meaning they are more likely to get big very quickly and could potentially spread to other parts of the brain or spinal cord. A brain tumour could start as a high grade or a low grade. If a low-grade tumour goes unnoticed, it could also turn into a high-grade tumour. Whatever is the history of the high-grade tumour, once it gets classified as 'high-grade', it receives the same treatment because being malignant, it poses a serious threat .

Glioblastoma

As mentioned earlier, amongst all the brain caners, the deadliest is called Glioblastoma Multiform or simply Glioblastoma or even simpler GBM.

Causes

What causes GBM, no body know and probably there is no point in speculating either and that's why global medical community is engaged in finding the cure instead of making futile attempts in investigating the causes. This is because there could be millions of reasons in our modern lifestyles that could be triggering it, ranging from radiations all around from devices such as mobiles, WiFi's, at homes and offices and ranging to environmental pollution, of all kind and everywhere. Also, since the genetic profiling of every human is different, and the tendency of every human is different in exposure of all the underlying potential causes, which makes finding the root cause almost an impossible job as well. At one point, 'genetic disorder' was a candidate for research of causes but is not being given much attention anymore; after it was established that the glioblastomas are *not* inherited.

That's the reason why the efforts are being channelized to find a cure, *if we can,* instead of wasting resources and time in finding the cause or causes. At moment, no treatment is showing any impressive results and that's the main reasons that all the statistics that are being published by the primary medical institutes of medical sciences in general and Neuropathy in specific are so grim.

Spread

Apart from the factors mentioned above that are common to all types of Brain Cancers, the GBM has an additional factor that makes it most malignant of all, which is its *aggressive* nature and the way it can aggressively infiltrate into surrounding, healthy regions of the brain.

Also, as per Dr Seckin Akgul at prescouter.com:

"Glioblastoma displays extreme degrees of genetic and phenotypic variations between tumours recovered from different patients. This important finding suggests that each patient has a different form of the disease and should therefore be treated according to unique features of their disease, as opposed to the standardized treatment strategies that we currently have."

Clearly, the key words above are *"each patient has a different form of the disease"*, and hence the challenges to the medical community to come up with one generic treatment.

Summary

The current treatment of GBM is no doubt enormously lacking in giving the desired positive results. Even though the current situation is grim, but that is not an end of the story. With the advancement in medical science and in information technology, hopes are there that in the near future, with the aid of sophisticated computers or may be through 'artificially intelligent' robots, customised treatment plans could be made for each GBM patients, because technology will give lot more assistance to the oncologists where conventional treatments failed.

Resources:

1)The Brain Tumour Charity, UK (www.thebraintumourcharity.org)
2)The American Brain Tumor Association (www.abta.org)
3) https://prescouter.com/2016/08/glioblastoma/

When Nature wants to drill a man
And thrill a man,
And skill a man,
When Nature wants to mould a man
To play the noblest part;
When she yearns with all her heart
To create so great and bold a man
That all the world shall praise-

Watch her method, watch her ways!
How she ruthlessly perfects
Whom she royally elects;
How she hammers him and hurts him
And with mighty blows converts him
Into trial shapes of clay which only Nature understands-

While his tortured heart is crying and he lifts beseeching hands! -
How she bends, but never breaks,
When his good she undertakes....
How she uses whom she chooses
And with every purpose fuses him,
By every art induces him
To try his splendor out-
Nature knows what she's about.

Excerpt from a Poem by
ANGELA MORGAN (1875 – 1957)

Printed in Great Britain
by Amazon

66594131R00200